THE DAVID HUME INSTITUTE 1989

# PROFESSIONAL LIABILITY: AN ECONOMIC ANALYSIS

THE DAVID HUME INSTITUTE

# Professional Liability: an Economic Analysis

Roger Bowles and Philip Jones

ABERDEEN UNIVERSITY PRESS
Member of Maxwell Macmillan Pergamon Publishing Corporation

First Published 1989
Aberdeen University Press
© The David Hume Institute 1989

**British Library Cataloguing in Publication Data**

Bowles, Roger A.
    Professional liability: an economic analysis.
      1. Professional personnel. Negligence. Liability–Law–
      Economic aspects.
      I. Title   II. Jones, Philip  III. David Hume Institute
      338.4'3342632

    ISBN 0 08 037962 1

PRINTED IN GREAT BRITAIN
THE UNIVERSITY PRESS
ABERDEEN

# Contents

# Figures and Tables

# Foreword

The efficient working of markets, as an instrument of consumer choice, presupposes that the consumer has full knowledge of the consequences of his/her choices, or that knowledge can be acquired quickly and easily if only by learning from one's mistakes. In the case of professional services, the consumer frequently cannot rely on his own expertise and may only seek them on rare but, for him or her, decisive occasions. Obtaining objective advice outside the professional cadres may be difficult and it is not unknown for professions to discourage even informative advertising by their own members. Therefore, once having chosen or accepted the source of professional advice, the consumer as client clearly seeks some assurance that the quality of service will be satisfactory, and that, if it turns out not to be so, some form of redress is open to him.

Messrs Bowles and Jones have made a special study of the important questions raised by professional liability for negligence. While it is accepted by such important professions as accountancy, architecture, law and medicine that the client must expect a high quality of service, the determination of the rules which should govern liability on grounds of negligence is a much-disputed matter. What the authors are concerned to show is that economic analysis has much to contribute towards the clarification of the issues surrounding the identification of professional liability, the calculation of its extent and the measures which might be adopted both to minimize professional negligence and to provide just compensation to those who suffer from it.

The Institute offers the usual disclaimer that it has no collective view on any subject treated in its publications, though it aims to publish only works of high quality which raise issues of public interest and concern. The work of Messrs Bowles and Jones is no exception to this rule. At the same time, the Institute welcomes this opportunity to make better known the economist's approach to what has been primarily regarded as a problem in legal philosophy.

Alan Peacock
Executive Director

# The Authors

**Roger Bowles and Philip Jones** are both Senior Lecturers in Economics at the University of Bath.

They have a special interest in the application of economics to legal problems.

# Acknowledgements

We are grateful to a number of people and organisations who have helped in the preparation of this paper. First and foremost we would like to thank Professor Sir Alan Peacock for suggesting that we write such a paper, for his encouragement and for his detailed and helpful comments on an earlier draft. We would like also to thank Noreen Welsh of the Law Society, the Institute of Chartered Accountants, the Association of Certified Accountants, Neil Pepperel and David Sinclair for providing us with various materials. The legal department of a Regional Health Authority made possible the empirical research reported in Chapter 2 and elsewhere. A number of academic colleagues, particularly participants in the Conference on Professional Liability organised by the Geneva Association in Geneva, Easter 1988 and the meeting of the European Association of Law and Economics held in September 1988 in Antwerp, made helpful comments on bits of the material at an earlier stage. Nancy Layton-Cook of Nelson Hurst & Marsh Ltd kindly gave us permission to reproduce the Proposal Form which appears in the Appendix to the Paper. Anne Swindells and Diana Monteiro provided efficient secretarial help.

Roger Bowles and Philip Jones
Bath, July 1989

# 1    Introduction

The object of this study is to explore an aspect of the provision of professional services which has become increasingly important in recent years. That is the question of the liability encountered by the professional in the event of making an error causing loss to his client or patient. In reviewing the arrangements covering a number of professions in the UK at present, we refer also to some of the significant reforms which have been mooted.

In the professions investigated in this paper the injured party relies on a negligence rule under which he can recover damages in respect of losses which can be demonstrated to be the consequence of a failure of a professional to act with a degree of care appropriate to a member of the profession. Within some of these professions however there are pressures for a move away from negligence, although as we will see the direction of change being urged differs widely. In the case of medicine for example the British Medical Association is pressing strongly for a 'no-fault' scheme under which the injured patient would be able to recover compensation provided he is able to demonstrate that the losses he has suffered are the consequence of medical treatment. This is an easier test to pass, since the patient is no longer in the rather invidious position of proving that his loss is the result of the acts or omissions of one or more identified individuals.

These sorts of moves can look very attractive on the surface: surely, one might argue, it would be sensible to make compensation depend on the loss the patient has suffered rather than having a 'forensic lottery' in which only those who can prove fault receive anything. As we shall see below, this kind of argument is a very narrow one and ignores many of the features of liability rules which are of importance from a resource allocation perspective. In this first chapter we outline an organising framework within which a broader view can be taken. It is constructed along the lines proposed by Calabresi in his important 1970 work (Calabresi, 1970) on the costs of accidents and extended later by a number of other authors (for a recent review of which see Stephen, 1988 or Shavell, 1987).

Before looking at this theoretical structure, we should perhaps make some comments on why we are seeking to develop an approach which can be applied equally to a set of activities as apparently diverse as accountancy, architecture, the law and medicine. The differences between these professional services, and the mechanisms through which they are provided, need little elaboration. They range from medicine, where services are provided to the public at zero user cost by practitioners who are paid a salary by the government, to accountancy and architecture where services are provided through private practitioners, with clients paying fees determined by demand and supply pressures in a market-place.

But the similarities are striking as well. The professional offers a service the quality of which may be difficult for the client to judge. Equally, the losses suffered in the event of errors being made by the practitioner may be very high, even terminal. It is thus important to the client that he should be offered, *ex ante*, assurances of high quality service. This may be achieved in various ways. It could be done, for example, purely by means of the practitioner's individual reputation. Alternatively a profession may operate a system of self-regulation in the hope of persuading the public that its practitioners are carefully selected, well trained and held accountable if their practice falls below the profession's own exacting standards. It may be done also by setting legally-enforceable standards, which, if not met, can result in public prosecution. A final means, and the one of central interest here, is a liability rule. Such rules are intended to leave the prospective client confident of redress, and can thus be interpreted as a device for underwriting a professional's promise of a high quality service.

The starting point for this work is the observation that a negligence rule is a central plank in the control of the quality of professional services across a wide range of activities. By creating incentives for the professional to take seriously the interests of the client, particularly when there may be a temptation to cut corners and relax the degree of care being exercised, it is possible that liability rules will be able to provide a degree of reassurance to clients which other institutions cannot match, at least at comparable cost.

## 1.1 An Evaluative Framework

Any system of dealing with accidents and their victims can be characterised by reference to a number of criteria. Accidents can be thought of in very general terms as unintended harmful consequences. For present purposes they can be taken to encompass any adverse outcome associated with making use of professional services. We will normally want to ask the following key questions of any system for dealing with accidents and errors:

(1) What degree of care will it induce those who may cause or contribute to accidents to exercise and what will be the cost of the accidents resulting from the exercise of a given degree of care?

(2) How are the losses caused by accidents spread amongst victims and others?

(3) How costly is the system to administer?

The answer to any one of these questions will not be decisive when it comes to evaluating alternative systems; rather, we shall be looking for the system which produces overall the best 'mix' of answers. A reform may look attractive in terms of one of these criteria but may be rejected because it measures up badly to another. For example, a system which is cheap to administer, might be rejected if it could be shown to produce an unacceptably high rate of accidents. Equally, a system producing a distribution of accident costs which is judged to be satisfactory might be rejected on the grounds that it is too complex and costly to administer.

The economic approach sets out to make the costs in each of the categories commensurable so that a judgement can, at least in principle, be reached as to the social optimum or best alternative. In practice of course it is very difficult to assign reliable estimates to the various categories of cost, but the great value of this approach is that it does at least enable us to identify some relevant questions. In the following sections we consider each of these questions in turn.

## 1.1.1 The degree of care and the costs of errors

The economic analysis of liability rules can be applied readily to the question of the choice of level of care exercised by a professional practitioner. The approach normally taken by analysts is to characterise the degree of care as an index. The economic agent is assumed to have sufficient knowledge to be able to translate his day-to-day actions into a measure of how likely it is that errors will result. The translation process may be only a relatively impressionistic kind of activity since care may have many dimensions and be difficult to summarise precisely as a single number. The important point is that the agent knows that by concentrating harder, working longer hours on a case, doing more preparatory work or whatever, he can reduce the probability of making a mistake and is in a position to exercise a degree of control over his own actions.

As a starting point consider Figure 1.1, taken from Bowles (1982). Exercising a higher degree of care reduces the likelihood of making errors so that the number and gravity of mistakes made, and thus the costs associated with them, decline as extra care is taken. This is illustrated by the cost of damage schedule (D) which is seen to decline as care is increased. The assumption usually made is that there are diminishing returns to care, i.e. that as more care is exercised the marginal gain (in terms of reduced harm) declines. A further common assumption, and one we also adopt, is that, even with the greatest care imaginable, some accidents will still happen. Our knowledge of how the world works is far from perfect, and all individuals are subject to limitations in their capacity to acquire and process all available information or to anticipate all possible contingencies.

Whatever else, we can be confident that it is costly to increase the degree of care being exercised. The professional will be able to provide fewer clients with services if he spends more time and trouble on each of the clients he takes on. Concentrating harder may be more tiring and lead the professional to seek compensation in the form of longer holidays or higher income. These kinds of effects are captured in the costs of care schedule (C) in Figure 1.1. The assumption usually made is that the costs of care are increasing with the degree of care and at an increasing rate. Increasing the degree of care imposes successively greater burdens at higher levels of care.

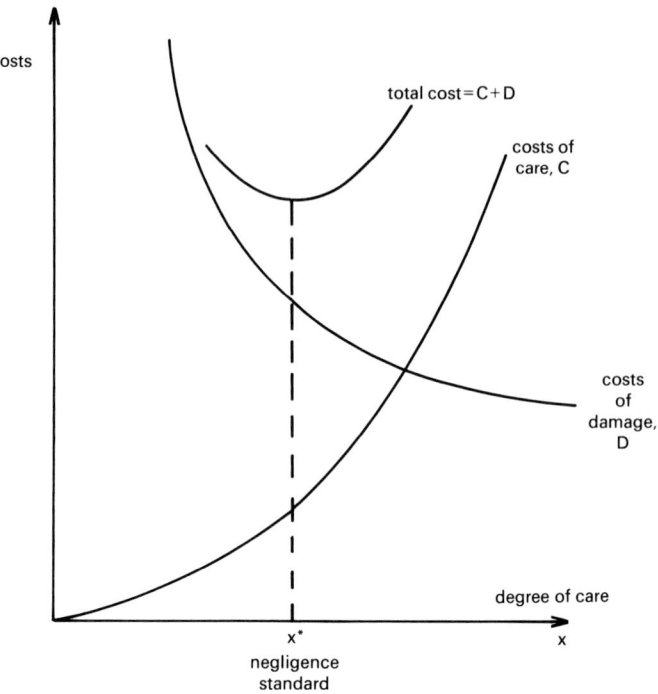

Figure 1.1   The efficient degree of care

The total cost of any degree of care can be thought of as the sum of the costs of damage and the costs of care. By adding the two schedules in Figure 1.1 which correspond with these two sets of costs we get the total cost of care schedule (C+D). The optimal degree of care can be inferred by finding the degree of care which minimises these total costs. In Figure 1.1 this level is x*. If less care than this is used some errors will be made which could have been prevented relatively cheaply, whereas any care beyond x* would have cost more than it saves in terms of accident reduction. For example, when people talk critically of 'defensive medicine' an economist would take them to mean that medical practitioners are taking steps which add little to patient safety and welfare whilst adding greatly to the cost of treatment.

Given that we can in this way identify the socially optimal degree of care, we ask next about the capacity of different liability rules to induce practitioners to choose that particular level. There are three kinds of liability rule which suggest themselves and we now consider each briefly.

### (a) No liability
If the practitioner is completely exempt from any liability then he need not worry about court actions on the part of clients whom he has harmed. The effect this has on the professional's behaviour will depend critically on the

degree to which information about the harm that he has caused finds reflection in the market's demand for his services. Prospective clients may be inclined to turn to other practitioners if and when news of his lapse reaches them. But if the news does not travel far, the influence on demand may be minimal. In the extreme case where nobody hears of the event, and the client involved was not a repeat customer, there may be no loss to the practitioner at all. At the other extreme where the news is loudly trumpeted the impact on market demand may be very large and may even force the practitioner out of business.

From the practitioner's point of view, economic analysis tells us that the degree of care he chooses will be influenced by the costs of damage and taking care as he perceives them. If errors never become public knowledge then the individual professional will have little or no incentive to exercise care so as to prevent them. Equally however if news of a single mistake could ruin a practice then we could expect the practitioner to exercise a very high degree of care. It is entirely possible that the practitioner might find he has an incentive to exercise care in excess of the level which would be chosen by reference to the private calculus of the client, if concern about reputational effects should predominate.

In theory then we would expect informational flows to be of central importance in determining behaviour in markets where there is no liability rule. Where information is thin, the fact that it is costly to take care will incline practitioners to economise on care and precautions, thus imposing heavy accident costs on hapless victims. Customers will be few and far between and the practitioner (and quite possibly the whole profession) will fall into disrepute, although it may still be patronised by the very poor or very desperate for whom a bad risk may be preferable to certain disaster. Backstreet abortionists, unlicensed doctors who treat injured criminals and jerry builders spring to mind as providers of services who exploit the lack of information in an environment where, for different reasons, they may be exempt from the usual pressures of professional liability. This argument is of course very similar to Akerlof's analysis of 'lemons': see Akerlof (1970). Markets for 'lemons', like second-hand cars, are liable to a comparable kind of informational failure. The seller has an incentive to withhold information from a prospective buyer. Prospective customers who see friends buying cars with unanticipated defects come to lose confidence in the goods and the market may collapse.

Care has to be taken not to exaggerate this argument. If prospective customers put sufficient value on the good or service, then sellers prepared to take care will have an incentive to advertise the fact. Similarly, the wary customer will be prepared to pay for information about the reliability of a trader or practitioner, making it potentially profitable for agents to compile and sell relevant information. Only in circumstances where it is extremely costly to provide the relevant flow of information is a complete collapse of the market likely.

In a well-established profession, the practitioner offering relatively lower quality services will find he loses clients to more careful colleagues to the extent that prospective clients are well-informed about variations between practitioners in the quality of service. To the extent that they may incur heavy losses by making a poor selection of practitioner, prospective customers will have an incentive to invest in acquiring information about accident records and so on. Equally, more careful practitioners will have an incentive to publicise their low accident rates. Therefore, one can argue, at least up to a point, that prospective clients will themselves be exercising care in their choice of practitioner.

There are indeed many economic activities which can function perfectly well in this way without any need for the paraphernalia of liability rules. An everyday example would be the entertainment industry. Cinema goers choose between the films they pay to go and see by talking to friends who have seen the film, or by reading publicity material, independent film reviews and so on. On the strength of this information they pay their entrance fee, but know perfectly well that they will sometimes be disappointed by what they see. Although in rare cases they may be so incensed that they demand a refund, they will normally just shrug and say something to the effect that some you win and some you lose.

The cinema owner may exercise some degree of control over his schedules so that he can build up a clientele who have confidence in his selections, and this is a further device that may simplify or cheapen the process of collecting information for the would-be film goer. There is not, however, any pressure for the introduction of a liability rule which would enable the customer to recover damages from the cinema owner in the event of being disappointed by a film. There are many other areas, however, in which liability rules do have a significant role to play. We shall argue that the provision of professional services is one area where liability rules may represent a superior means of conveying both information and reassurance to prospective clients who might otherwise lack confidence in the quality of service to be expected from a particular practitioner or profession.

### (b) Negligence

All the professions we examine in later chapters are subject to liability on the basis of negligence. The diagrammatic treatment in Figure 1.1 can be readily adapted to show the effects of a negligence-based liability rule on the incentive structure facing the professional. In Figure 1.2 we indicate that the income-maximising practitioner will have incentives to take the efficient degree of care, provided that the standard of care legally required corresponds with the efficient (i.e. cost-minimising) degree of care.

If the professional fails to exercise care to the level required, then he is normally responsible for paying damages to the client in respect of the losses thereby occasioned. His total costs when setting the level of care below $x^*$ (Figure 1.2) are thus given as the sum of the costs of care and the costs of accidents caused. But provided that care taken is $x^*$ or higher, then he is no longer liable for the cost of accidental damage caused. From that point on therefore he need worry only about the costs of care. Since we have assumed these to be increasing, the rational professional will thus choose to exercise care

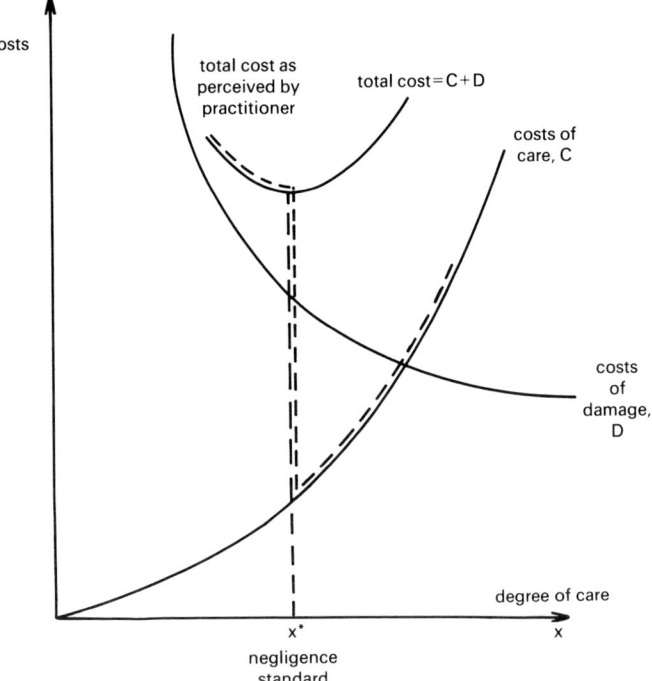

costs

total cost as perceived by practitioner

total cost = C + D

costs of care, C

costs of damage, D

degree of care

x*    x

negligence standard

Figure 1.2    Choice of level of care under a negligence rule

at the efficient level. Below x* costs increase sharply because of damage costs whilst above x* costs increase due to the rising cost of care.

As far as the consumer is concerned we may interpret the position as follows. Should the practitioner fail to exercise care at a level x* or higher, the practitioner will be responsible for the losses. The customer will still himself be liable for the losses which result when the practitioner is exercising due care. In everyday terms this means that the customer may find it advisable to take insurance cover against the risks which he faces, i.e. the risks which remain even when the practitioner is exercising reasonable care. Our understanding of the world is imperfect, and even the most careful of practitioners will sometimes be unable to avoid causing loss. Under a negligence rule, therefore, we could say that risks are shared. The customer pays if the losses arise in circumstances where the practitioner is sufficiently careful, but the practitioner (or his insurer) indemnifies the customer for losses should they result from a failure of the practitioner to excercise reasonable care. It is worth mentioning also that we would expect very few claims for negligence actually to be initiated under a negligence rule, since the professional would always choose a degree of care sufficient to avoid liability.

### (c) Strict liability
Under a strict liability rule the practitioner is required to compensate the customer for any loss, irrespective of whether it is the product of carelessness.

This rule has a simple interpretation in diagrammatic terms, since the professional becomes liable for all losses and thus faces a total costs schedule $(C+D)$ identical with the total costs incorporated in Figure 1.1. It follows immediately that the rational professional will choose to exercise the socially efficient level of care, $x^*$, since that is the one which maximises his own level of income.

The professional's costs of practising will accordingly be higher under this strict liability approach than under negligence, since he has now become responsible for the costs of accidents occurring whatever degree of care is exercised. The fees he charges will be higher to enable him to cover these additional costs, whilst the customer will be making corresponding savings by no longer being responsible for any losses at all.

These findings are entirely consistent with the well-known Coase Theorem which states that the allocation of resources will be independent of who bears the losses from harmful activities. In a more familiar setting of conflicts over land use it does not matter whether the farmer whose crops are destroyed or the railroad responsible for the sparks which damage crops is made responsible for the losses. Efficient bargaining between the parties, provided it is costless, will ensure that the cost-minimising arrangement of the two activities will be produced. Imposing liability on the farmer will give him an incentive to 'buy off' railroad activities so long as the losses experienced by the farmer exceed the costs to the railroad of reducing services.

In the context of professional services there is no conflict over resource use, but simply a conflict of interest over how careful the practitioner is to be. An efficient solution of the conflict can be achieved equally well by a strict liability rule or a negligence rule. It may therefore be tempting to conclude that on pure efficiency grounds there is nothing to choose between the two rules. In practice, however, there may be other elements figuring in incentive structures sufficient to tip the balance one way or the other on purely efficiency grounds. As we have already emphasised there will be concerns beyond the choice of degree of care by the professional which influence the final choice between liability rules. But for the moment we shall only consider possible impediments to the achievement of efficiency under the two rules being examined.

## 1.1.2 Possible sources of inefficiency

Just as there are cases where the Coase Theorem does not operate fully (e.g. because of the existence of positive bargaining costs) so too there may be barriers to the achievement of an efficient allocation of resources under one or more of the liability rules with which we are concerned. From an analytical perspective most of these barriers will be manifest in the form of a distortion of the link between the degree of care exercised and the costs the practitioner faces. Not all distortions of these relationships will necessarily affect the practitioner's choice of degree of care, but many will.

Let us consider an example in detail. For the legal practitioner, the argument thus far concludes that under either a negligence rule or a strict liability rule the lawyer will choose to practice with degree of care x* (Figure 1.2). In order for this result to hold we need to satisfy a number of conditions, and in particular the following.

### (a) The standard of care

First, the court must be able to identify the efficient level of care and to determine reliably whether a lawyer's actions fall short of this standard, so that under a negligence approach the lawyer will minimise his costs at x*. In practice courts will base their enquiries on whether other (reasonable) members of the profession would have taken the same steps as the lawyer who is being sued. This approach will achieve the desired end only as long as the profession as a whole is making decisions which are consistent with the efficiency solution x*. It is not always clear whether (or even why) this should be the case.

Another possible impediment results from the role of insurance. Since claims against practitioners tend to be large and unevenly spread through time and, since practitioners will often be risk averse, there is naturally scope for the creation of an insurance market. Professional indemnity insurance has expanded rapidly in the UK over the past decade as claims have risen. Professions, anxious in part to reassure clients, have in a number of cases moved to make evidence of liability insurance a pre-condition of continuing membership.

However, once insured, the practitioner's incentive to exercise care may be reduced. This 'moral hazard' problem is familiar from other insurance markets. The householder with a contents policy, for example, is less careful about locking doors and windows than his neighbour who has not bought such a policy. Similarly, the professional with an insurance policy indemnifying him against the costs of liability claims may perceive a reduction in the costs of inflicting harm. For the practitioner, a successful claim against him for negligence may still entail time-consuming and embarrassing correspondence and court appearances but it will not spell disaster. In the longer term this may influence his indemnity insurance premiums, his capacity for promotion and so on, but in the short term there will be few if any effects on his income level.

Insurance companies are of course fully aware of these problems and have incentives to find ways of minimising such risks to their profitability. Central to these efforts are devices to screen applicants to establish how careful they have been in the past and to create disincentives to being careless in the form of 'experience rating' of premiums and the use of 'deductibles'. Experience rating involves adjustments to premiums in relation to claims experience in previous years whilst deductibles require the practitioner to bear the first £x of any loss.

### (b) The quantum of damages

Secondly, we have also to assume that the court makes an accurate assessment of the amount, or technically the *quantum* of damages. If the court underestimates or overestimates the amount of harm being done then the costs of harm schedule as perceived by the professional will be distorted and may lead to the choice of a degree of care which is not the one which minimises total costs. The grounds for suspecting that the amount recovered by injured clients understates losses are various.

The more likely possibilities can be derived from an analysis of the incentive (under a negligence rule) to litigate confronting an injured party. Suppose the client's loss resulting from the professional's alleged error to be £10,000. The client estimates the cost of a legal action seeking compensation to be £4,000. The probability of succeeding in court is 60 per cent, in which case the client will recover the £10,000 to cover his losses plus £4,000 costs.

The defendant of the claim has the opportunity, under English law, to make an offer to the plaintiff to settle the claim before trial. If the plaintiff rejects the offer he becomes responsible for both his own costs and the costs of the defendant from the date of offer to the date of trial. This procedural rule has the intention of promoting settlements rather than costly trials. But from the plaintiff's perspective it has the following effect. The expected recovery is £6,000 (= probability of 0.6 multiplied by damages of £10,000). An offer to settle the case for much less than this amount will however very often succeed.

Assume that half the legal costs are incurred prior to the offer to settle and half incurred at trial. Assume also that the defendant's costs are similar. The defendant (D) calculates that the plaintiff (P) is in the following position. If P wins he recovers his £10,000 and incurs no costs. If he loses at trial he recovers zero damages, incurs his own additional (i.e. post-offer) trial costs of £2,000 and has to indemnify the defendant for his costs of £2,000. The gamble for the plaintiff involves therefore a 60 per cent chance of winning £10,000 and a 40 per cent chance of losing £4,000. The rational defendant will not have to make a very generous offer in such circumstances, since he can to a large degree rely on the plaintiff's aversion to risk. Even a risk neutral plaintiff will settle for £4,400 in these circumstances where the actuarial value of the claim is £6,000, while a risk averse individual might settle for considerably less, say £2–2,500.

Since defendants in professional liability cases will generally be insurance companies who are well able to diversify risk and have a strong incentive to be well-informed about the likely outcome of trials, low offers to settle can be expected ('low' here referring to the size of offer relative to the amount of damages the court would decide). If professional indemnity insurance premiums are closely tailored to such costs, as there is every reason to suppose they will be, then the costs faced by the professional may significantly understate the losses to clients. The costs of administering indemnity policies will of course operate in the reverse direction, by inflating the costs perceived by the practitioner relative to the amounts awarded to injured clients. The net effect will be difficult to estimate in practice, but the possibility of a divergence between the harm experienced by clients and the costs of harm as perceived by the professional is clear.

In order to demonstrate the consequences of this let us assume, as is commonly argued, that injured parties do not generally received an award of damages sufficient to compensate them for their losses. In Figure 1.3 we illustrate this assumption by drawing the costs of harm schedule below the position it would occupy were losses fully compensated. We are assuming

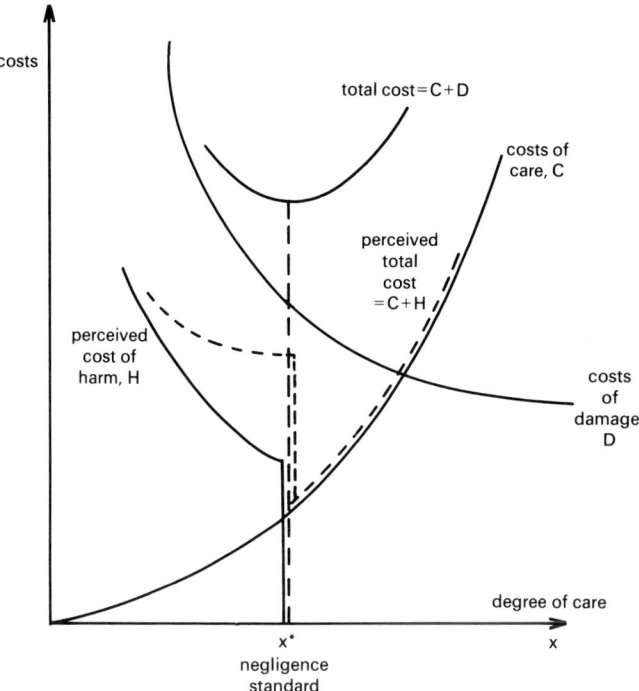

Figure 1.3    Choice of level of care under a negligence rule with undercompensation

implicitly here that the degree of undercompensation is proportional to the amount of harm caused.

Under a negligence rule, this displacement has no effect on the choice of level of care, since from the practitioner's point of view the minimum cost degree of care is still x*. Thus while clients are being undercompensated in circumstances where negligent errors occur, the lawyer will still normally face an incentive to exercise a degree of care x*.

Under a strict liability rule, by contrast, the displacement of the costs of damage schedule has the effect of displacing the total perceived costs schedule which will now reach a minimum at a point to the left of x*. Thus as well as clients being undercompensated, we have the second and possibly more serious effect of creating incentives for lawyers to exercise less care and thus to cause more accidents.

### (c) Perceptions of the costs of care

A third condition which may not be satisfied in practice is the assumption that the cost of care as perceived by practitioners is an accurate reflection of the true cost. The most vivid example of this comes from the medical area. The doctor employed by the NHS treating a patient in hospital may consider doing diagnostic tests. In current conditions it is very unlikely that, even if he were to ask, he would be able to find out the cost of the test.

The decision about whether to run the test can be thought of in terms of how careful the practitioner intends to be. He will not be in a position to make cost-minimising decisions in practice if the costs cannot be discovered. It could be argued that the doctor will treat the tests as 'free', in which case he will tend to make profligate use of them. In reality, of course, there will be devices which encourage him to economise on testing. Constraints on the capacity of the pathology laboratory, for example, will mean that restrictions will be imposed with testing facilities being unavailable or turnround time being such that the doctor judges there to be no point in applying. Hospitals in Bath for example do not offer a blood testing service for outpatients on Mondays.

Whilst it is possible to argue that UK medical practitioners may lack incentives to economise on testing, there is a certain irony in the observation that in the US doctors, who are probably much more conscious of the costs of tests, engage in rather more testing. In the folklore this is ascribed to the doctor's defence strategy against the greater propensity on the part of American patients to litigate.

In other professions this ignorance of the costs of care is probably less wide-spread. Professional firms in the UK are for the most part organised as partner-ships. The practitioner's income is thus sensitive to the costs of running the practice as well as to the revenue it generates. Additional care raises costs, and may reduce revenue if it involves dealing with a smaller number of clients. The point is that the profit-sharing partner is concerned with net income, and this encourages him to take seriously both the costs of harm and the costs of care. The salaried professional may be less immediately conscious of the costs to the firm of his taking additional care, although in a profit-maximising firm, in which his behaviour is monitored effectively, he will quickly be told if he is taking 'too much' care.

From a pure efficiency standpoint, these various sources of incongruence between costs as they appear to the professional and costs as they appear to society are a matter for concern since they may inhibit the system's capacity to achieve the desired degree of care. In practice, it will thus be important to ask two questions. First, are conditions in a profession such that practitioners face a pattern of incentives likely to point them in the right direction? And secondly, is one liability rule likely to be more robust than another in terms of its capacity to deal with incongruences between privately-perceived costs and real social costs? The first of these questions is the subject matter of later chapters. We would conjecture that the answer to the second is that a negligence rule shows signs of greater robustness since it imposes an external requirement on the degree of care and this is likely to be reflected, at least to some degree, in the private cost-benefit calculus of the professional.

This completes our analysis of the efficiency dimension of professional liability. To summarise our position, we have argued that a liability rule of some description is likely to be found in professional services because it reassures prospective clients about the quality of service or care they can expect and as a result enables them to keep to a minimum the amount of information they need to gather before choosing a practitioner. The choice between a strict liability rule and a negligence rule is a matter of indifference so long as it is possible to confront practitioners with an appropriate set of incentives. Where this is difficult, our suggestion would be that a negligence rule is likely to be the more reliable of the two. But as we have already argued, these efficiency arguments are only a part of the story. In the following sections 1.2 and 1.3 we examine the other two of the three elements which go into any evaluation of a system for controlling errors.

## 1.2   Loss-spreading

Losses suffered by people as a result of the acts or omissions of a professional practitioner can be dealt with, or distributed, in various ways. The client can be made responsible, the professional can be made responsible or the costs can be absorbed by a wider group. Different approaches to liability therefore give rise to different distributions of the burden of loss, and these differences are likely to be a significant element in the final choice of liability rule. As in the previous section we proceed by looking in turn at each of three possible regimes.

### (a) No liability

In the absence of a liability rule the losses are borne directly by those clients who incur damage. The person buying a poorly-designed house finds his assets diminish in value; the injured patient has to suffer loss of income while he receives new treatment and so on. Clients may of course buy first party insurance to protect themselves against such loss, and thus spread the risks among themselves. Provided that insurance markets are functioning properly there should be no problems with this kind of solution: the housebuyer takes out a policy under which his house is rebuilt if it turns out to be defective and the worker takes out a health policy which replaces income lost as a result of injuries received.

There may also exist institutions which spread some of the risks more widely. In the UK the well-developed social security system plays an important part as does public provision of health services. The injured patient for example receives free hospital treatment and quite probably state-provided sick pay while off work. To some degree, therefore, the costs of accidents caused by professionals are met not by their clients but by the taxpayer at large.

The price they are prepared to pay for professional services will reflect the extent to which clients can expect to be left with losses. The greater the expected loss, the greater the cost of buying first party insurance and thus the lower the price they are prepared to pay for professional services. This will be most serious in circumstances where for some reason insurance markets do not work very well. If the number of risks is very small, potential losses very large or the control of moral hazard difficult, then it may be impossible or extremely costly to buy insurance. This will mean in turn that the client who cannot insure faces the prospect of catastrophic loss and thus turns away from making use of the services of a professional. The individual's capacity to absorb risk may be very limited, so that if first party insurance is not available, the absence of a liability rule may prompt the collapse of the professional's market.

### (b) Negligence rule

Under a negligence rule clients receive compensation for any loss which can be shown to be the result of a practitioner's negligence. The client remains responsible for losses which result in circumstances where the practitioner has acted in a way regarded as reasonable for a member of his profession. From a distributive perspective this has some good points and some drawbacks.

On the plus side, the client benefits from a degree of insurance against loss through the fee he pays the professional. It may well be cheaper for the professional to insure these losses than the client. There are likely to be many more clients than professionals, so that fewer insurance policies have to be written for the same degree of coverage. Anything which helps insurance companies economise on their administrative costs is likely to reduce premiums, so that the implicit premium the client pays through his fee will be lower than the premium he would have to pay for comparable first party cover. Insurance costs may also be lower because the insurance company will generally be able to monitor and control its risk exposure more effectively if the insurance contract is with the producer rather than the consumer.

On the negative side, there is the difficulty that two clients suffering the same loss, where one is the result of negligence and the other is not, will not recover the same amount of damages from the professional. This inequity is probably more apparent than real. If the client is properly insured, i.e. has first party insurance to cover losses which cannot be attributed to negligence, then it should not make any difference. The two clients will both be fully compensated for their loss, but will recover the losses through different channels, one from his own insurer and the other from the insurer of the professional.

### (c) Strict liability

Under a strict liability rule the client is compensated for all losses by the professional or the professional's insurer. This solution is convenient for the client who need not take out any first party cover, and thus results in a minimum number of insurance contracts being required. It also has the advantage that all clients are seen to be evenly treated.

## 1.3 Administrative Costs

The third component in an assessment of the alternative approaches to professional liability entails an analysis of the costs of administering the different arrangements. In the absence of a liability rule these costs will be zero but under either strict liability or negligence they may be substantial. It is useful to begin with an analysis of the distinction between issues of liability and of quantum.

### 1.3.1 Establishing liability

Taking first the issue of liability, the parties (or failing that, the court or whatever forum is specified) have to decide whether the professional is to be held responsible for the losses at issue. Under strict liability the professional will be liable to meet losses incurred by the client where it can be established that the losses at issue are a consequence of the service provided and would not have occurred otherwise. This may sound like a fairly innocuous test, although in practice it may be more onerous. In the medical area, for example, a patient would have to show that he has suffered loss as a result of treatment received and would not have suffered the same losses had the treatment not been given. These sorts of decisions are usually referred to a social security style of tribunal which concerns itself with the question of whether the plaintiff can establish entitlement to compensation.

Of course, under negligence the plaintiff confronts the much more difficult task of proving to the court that a professional failed to exercise the reasonable degree of care expected from members of the profession and that he has suffered loss as a consequence. There are two possibly troublesome elements here. First the plaintiff has to establish what actually happened and what was the cause of loss. He is at a severe informational disadvantage at this stage since he does not have access to the professional's knowledge or notes on events. By using discovery procedures he can, through the court, require the professional to disclose notes and records but he may need considerable knowledge and professional advice in order to ask the right questions and to obtain the relevant documents. The plaintiff then has to establish that the professional did not act reasonably. This will normally entail taking an opinion from another professional as to how a reasonably competent practitioner would have behaved in the circumstances.

The plaintiff may therefore incur heavy expenses in establishing that the professional is liable. He has no guarantee that he will succeed in this task, and is unlikely to be able to recover his costs in the event of failure. From a social cost perspective it does not matter that in the UK the plaintiff may be legally-aided since the resources allocated to the enquiry are real resources with an opportunity cost which has to be met by someone.

## 1.3.2 Quantum

Having once established liability the question of quantifying loss arises. There is generally room for dispute about the appropriate amount, since losses may spread into the future, and some decision will have to be taken based on an appropriate prognosis. The civil courts which hear claims for negligence have well established methods for calculating losses, so that experienced lawyers should be able to estimate with reasonable accuracy how much a court would award in any particular case.

Under strict liability the question of quantum may, like the question of liability, be decided by a small tribunal rather than a full-blown court. This is likely to be a considerably cheaper forum, although as usual there may be drawbacks. The tribunal will almost certainly use a simpler means of calculating compensation, and, to protect injured parties from feeling aggrieved by apparently arbitrary decisions, it may well be necessary to allow the parties recourse to the courts should they wish to appeal against a tribunal's decision.

The net result is that in any given case of loss a strict liability rule will enable a resolution at considerably lower cost than a negligence rule. The determination of liability under negligence is a costly affair. However, to set against this higher cost per case is the certainty that there will be more claims under a strict liability rule. More injured parties will file claims and fewer of those who file claims will lose on the question of liability. This is likely to put heavy pressure on those who are underwriting the compensation payments unless some means are found to limit the compensation fund's budget. The suggestion is, for example, that a 'no-fault' scheme for victims of medical accidents would be constrained to make much smaller payments than would be awarded by a court applying the normal principles of damages. This would of course have the effect of forcing the client back into the market for first party insurance as well as subverting the system's capacity to bring about the efficient degree of care.

## 1.4 Concluding Remarks

The preceding sections have outlined a framework within which the institution of professional liability can be analysed. There is no straightforward decision rule which can be deduced to choose once and for all between the alternative liability regimes. There is a tension between the meeting of different objectives, and, since professions differ, the trade-offs will take different forms so that there may well be differences in the optimal form of liability regime. Thus we need to consider each profession in turn on its merits before we can expect to reach a sensible conclusion as to how best to deal with those of its customers who incur loss.

The professions we examine in the following chapters are all covered at present by a system of negligence-based liability. There are differences between professions in the degree to which the indemnity insurance premium paid by a practitioner is related to the number of claims he experiences, and to some degree there are differences also in the stringency of the legal test applied in determining whether an action is to be classed as negligent.

Within a number of the professions, particularly architecture and medicine, there has been significant pressure for substantial modification to the current negligence approach. The British Medical Association were (at least until recently) pressing for the introduction of a 'no-fault' or strict liability regime, under which more injured patients would receive smaller amounts of compensation. Architects are pressing for a shift to a no liability system in which the client has to make his own arrangements for meeting loss. In the different chapters we will look at some of these proposals in more detail, having first said something about each profession and how it works.

# 2   Medical Negligence

## 2.1   Introduction

In Chapter 1 we introduced a framework for an analysis of professional liability. Here the intention is to apply this same set of criteria to those procedures which have evolved for dealing with negligence in the medical profession. The questions to be raised are, therefore, essentially those which are implied by the criteria of Calabresi (1970).

For example, we ask first whether the current system of actions brought for negligence provides the 'educative' or 'deterrent' function which has been deemed desirable. Will doctors learn from negligence and will they have an incentive to choose an 'efficient' level of care? How will current arrangements ensure that 'correct' signals are conveyed to doctors and what incentive mechanisms exist to ensure that this information plays a role in their decision making? Such mechanisms are essential if the negligence system is to stimulate an efficient use of resources.

However, there is also the second issue of whether the present negligence system provides adequate redress or compensation to those who suffer injuries as a result of medical treatment. Will those who suffer medical negligence have access to the courts and will they win damages commensurate with their losses? If not, would a different approach to liability (e.g. a no-fault scheme) have superior properties?

Finally, will this whole procedure imply 'excessive' administrative and legal costs? Are there less expensive ways of achieving the goals of efficiency and equity? It is obviously desirable that such transactions costs be kept to a minimum and here we seek to compare the administrative and legal costs of the current system of negligence with those of possible alternative arrangements.

In order to apply the analysis of Chapter 1, we begin by describing the way in which the medical profession in the UK has responded to the question of professional liability. As indicated in Chapter 1, paragraph 1, the law of negligence allows plaintifs to bring medical malpractice suits to the courts in an attempt to prove negligence. Doctors safeguard their position by purchasing indemnity insurance. However, in recent years there has been a considerable escalation in medical litigation in the UK and the rather anachronistic arrangements which have characterised the system of medical negligence to date are now under pressure.

## 2.2  Professional Indemnity Insurance for Medical Negligence

In the UK, professional indemnity insurance is acquired by doctors through membership of one of three medical defence societies. In England and Wales doctors tend to be members of either the Medical Defence Union or the Medical Protection Society. Scottish doctors (or those qualifying in Scotland) may be members of the Medical and Dental Defence Union of Scotland. Medical defence societies are non-profit organisations which provide advisory services to members as well as indemnity insurance. In the event of malpractice suits being brought against members, the legal costs and any damages are met by the medical defence society. Doctors employed by the National Health Service are required to have indemnity insurance. General practitioners recover this expenditure as a part of their practice expenses, though, of course, the cash flow of the practice is reduced. Health authorities are vicariously liable for hospital doctors in certain circumstances. Negligence claims are typically brought against the health authority, in the first instance, but if the injured patient can demonstrate that his losses are the result of a named doctor's negligence rather than, say, of poorly managed facilities, then the doctor's defence society assumes liability. Hospital doctors have long been able to set these indemnity insurance costs against income tax. However, with the recent escalation of costs of subscription, the NHS has been made to reimburse two thirds of these costs for doctors employed full-time by the NHS

The growth in insurance premiums for doctors is shown in Table 2.1. The rise in subscription reflects a growth in claims frequency and claims severity over this period. The number of medical malpractice claims per annum has doubled during the 1980s. Average awards for medical negligence are currently between £10,000 and £20,000 and the highest sum awarded in a medical negligence case has risen from £132,970 in 1977 to £1,03 million in 1987. The rise in average awards is said to be mirrored by the rise in maximum awards. This is shown in Figure 2.1.

The arrangements for dealing with medical malpractice have important implications for the supply of medical care and for the budgets of the National Health Service. In 1986–7 the health authorities paid a total of £9.3 million as compensation for losses. The answer to a recent Parliamentary question in the House of Commons shows the incidence of claims in excess of £100,000 to be rising rapidly; see Table 2.2.

It is not surprising, therefore, that the question has been raised as to whether the UK is heading towards a 'crisis' situation, similar to the medical malpractice problem which has plagued the USA for some time. But the rate of growth of claims in the UK (at little more than 1 per cent per annum) is reported by Quam et al. (1987) to have been much slower than the growth rate in the USA (15 per cent per annum). It is not necessary, therefore, to be too alarmist about the scale of the problem.

Nevertheless, with the costs of medical negligence escalating, there is considerable concern as to the adequacy of present arrangements to cope with increasing pressures. Will the current system for furnishing professional indemnity insurance in the UK be robust in the face of rapidly rising claims?

*Table 2.1*    MEDICAL DEFENCE ORGANISATION SUBSCRIPTIONS 1980–9

| Year | Full subscription, £, current prices | Full subscription £, 1980 prices |
|------|--------------------------------------|----------------------------------|
| 1980 | 95 | 95 |
| 1981 | 120 | 107 |
| 1982 | 135 | 111 |
| 1983 | 195 | 156 |
| 1984 | 264 | 198 |
| 1985 | 288 | 204 |
| 1986 | 336 | 230 |
| 1987 | 576 | 378 |
| 1988 | 1080 | 677 |
| 1989 | 1350* | 806** |

\*    Figure for 1989 announced by Medical Defence Union, November 1988
\*\*   Assumes 5 per cent inflation mid 1988–mid 1989

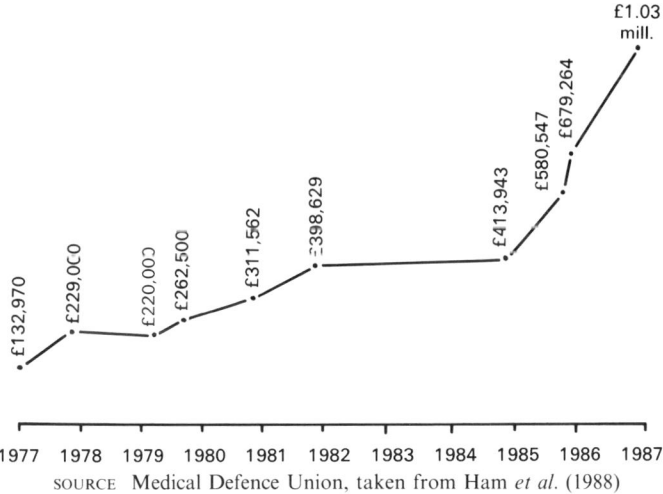

SOURCE   Medical Defence Union, taken from Ham *et al.* (1988)

Figure 2.1    Highest sum awarded in medical negligence cases

Is there a need to reform or replace the present system of negligence? It is perhaps to be expected that, in the face of both a growth of claims frequency and awards, the medical profession and the NHS would be drawn to reconsider the virtues of present arrangements. Indeed, the British Medical Association has gone as far as to recommend the introduction of a system of no-fault, whereby eligibility for compensation would not be dependent upon individuals proving medical negligence in the law courts (Bolt, 1989).

*Table 2.2* COMPENSATION PAYMENTS IN EXCESS OF £100,000 MADE BY HEALTH
AUTHORITIES, 1982–7

| Year and Health Authority | Amount of award/ settlement (£) |
| --- | --- |
| 1982–3 | |
| — | — |
| 1983–4 | |
| Croydon | 250,000 |
| Swindon | 534,000 |
| 1984–5 | |
| Hounslow and Spelthorne | 220,760 |
| Islington | 235,000 |
| 1985–6 | |
| Bassetlaw | 385,000 |
| Grimsby | 270,000 |
| Solihull | 250,000 |
| Swindon | 275,000 |
| 1986–7 | |
| Bath | 175,000 |
| Cambridge | 151,222 |
| Central Birmingham | 175,000 |
| Central Manchester | 207,000 |
| East Berkshire | 550,000 |
| North Lincolnshire | 130,000 |
| Nottingham | 115,000 |
| Nottingham | 375,000 |
| Walsall | 260,000 |
| Wandsworth | 600,000 |
| West Surrey and North East Hampshire | 150,498 |
| 1987–8 | |
| Bloomsbury | 430,000 |
| Crewe | 375,000 |
| Torbay | 350,000 |

NOTE   The figures shown represent the total amount of the award/settlement, excluding costs.
They do not take account of the fact that the health authority's liability may have been
reduced by a contribution from a medical defence organisation.
SOURCE   Hansard 27 May 1988 cc 409–10

## 2.3   The 'Educative' Role of Negligence

The theoretical analysis of negligence presented in Chapter 1 can be applied to
the current procedures for medical negligence. In order to appraise any liability
arrangement, we outline the workings of a negligence system in an 'ideal'
market environment. Deviations from the 'ideal' may then be highlighted and
assessed. Initially, the focus of our discussion rests on those factors which must
be present if the educative function is to be achieved. If professionals are to
make 'efficient' decisions, signals from the tort system must be accurate and

must be effective within those incentive mechanisms which guide the decisions of practitioners.

Foremost amongst those conditions required to achieve the 'educative' role of negligence is that court awards for damages are set 'correctly'. Courts must be sufficiently well informed to determine the costs of negligence if appropriate signals are to be sent to decision takers. In the case of medical malpractice, Schwartz and Komesar (1978) argue that signals guide an efficient use of resources provided that awards are set by courts according to the losses that the patient might experience as a consequence of negligence. To relate this to judicial practice, reference is often made to the definition of negligence as laid down by Judge Learned Hand in the USA. Following this definition of losses, the ruling established a definition of negligence as having occurred 'if the loss caused by accident, multiplied by the probability of the accident's occurring, exceeds the burden of the precautions the defendant might have taken to avert it' (Danzon, 1988, p 15). It can be shown that this principle accords well with an 'efficient' use of resources, if used to guide court awards.

Figure 2.2 is derived from the analysis in Chapter 1. The marginal benefits to any patient of additional professional care can be thought of as the amount which a patient would be willing to pay to reduce the expected costs of damages that he can expect when purchasing these services. However, as shown in Chapter 1, a liability rule will make these costs of damages the concern of the practitioner. In so far as the practitioner is ultimately liable (through the courts) for these damages, the marginal benefit function (MB) in Figure 2.2 may be thought of as the value of additional care to the practitioner in reducing his exposure to expected damage costs. The marginal benefits of additional care (i.e. the reduction in expected damage costs), may occur either because additional care reduces the probability of a particular accident or because it alters the nature of the problem and, thereby, decreases the costs of the accident which may result. Reductions in expected damages costs are assumed to decline with additional care, while in Figure 2.2, the marginal costs of care (MC) i.e. the value of the additional resources, are likely to increase with additional care. Provided that court awards of damages reflect fully the losses to those who suffer, it will be in the interests of the practitioner to increase care provided the marginal costs of additional medical care are less than the reduction in the expected damages as a result of negligence (i.e. the marginal benefits to the practitioner of additional medical care). By this procedure the practitioner will be led to a level of care indicated by $x^*$.

In this process it is evident that 'efficiency' in resource allocation has been attained, to the extent that the marginal benefits to patients of additional medical care are equated to the additional resource costs of medical care. By comparison with the analysis in Chapter 1, the combined cost of expected damages and medical care is minimised. Moreover, it is clear that solution $x^*$ is in the spirit of the judgement of Judge Learned Hand. Beyond $x^*$ no negligence has occurred; the additional costs of attempting to avoid the accident are not warranted by the expected loss associated with not incurring them. Therefore, provided that the standards of professional practice evolve so as to minimise costs of damages and costs of medical care, the issue of liability

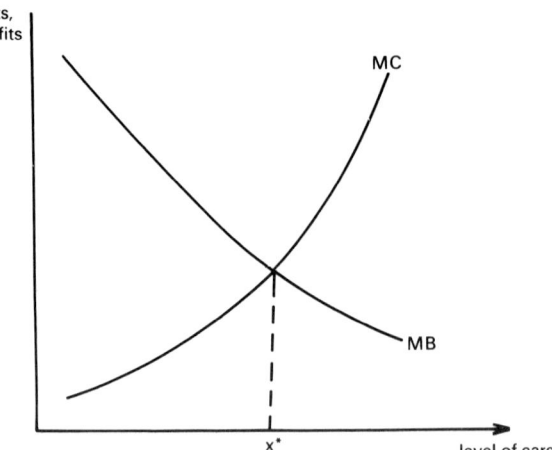

Figure 2.2    The efficient level of care

is only relevant if the practitioner reduces his level of care below x*. As long as he provides a quality of service to the standards that might reasonably be expected of his peers he would not be liable to negligence. Also, as long as he perceives the true costs of damages and medical care, he would regret not choosing to practise at x* if he were ever called to account, i.e. there would be a deterrent to choosing any level of care below x*.

Of course, one of the problems of current arrangements is that the practitioner appears insulated from the marginal expected costs of damages by indemnity insurance. This creates the possibility of moral hazard. If the practitioner is covered against losses and, if his insurance premium does not depend upon his actions directly, then it may be less expensive for the practitioner to choose not to incur the cost of precaution; knowing that he is insulated from any such losses which may arise as a result of having insurance cover. However, there are well known mechanisms by which insurance agencies can reduce moral hazard. The use of deductibles, whereby the insured party pays the first portion of any loss is one example. More generally, however, the problem can be resolved if insurance premiums are adjusted perfectly to relate to the prospects that each insured person will incur a claim. In this way, by engaging in those costs which reduce the probability of a loss, the insured party can expect some benefit in terms of a reduced insurance premium.[1]

If premiums were to reflect perfectly the expected future losses then the behaviour of the insured would directly affect his premium. Ideally insurance premiums would be perfectly premised upon a set of attributes which would relate to the expected future costs of each doctor. It is common, for example, for motor car insurance premiums to be based on factors such as the car's make and whether the car is kept in a garage. Some of the motorist's characteristics (like age and occupation) will play a part as well. Such information is used as a proxy for expected future claims on the policy. Often a history of claims is taken as a predictor of future claims. In this respect a direct incentive is created for the insured party to behave in a non-negligent fashion.

The incentive to act in a non-negligent fashion is the mechanism by which the marginal benefit function in Figure 2.2 is made relevant to the decision taker. The question with which we are now faced is whether, with reference to medical negligence in the UK, there is any reason to suppose that under current arrangements such a signal will be distorted or attenuated. There is certainly reason to suppose that the signal which is transmitted via insurance premiums *can* be made relevant to the practitioner. Indeed, there has on occasion been concern that, if the damages costs were set 'too high' it might induce a tendency for 'over use' of medical care and for 'defensive medicine'. While it is difficult to prove that medical practice is excessively careful it is difficult also to prove how widespread is the prevalence of 'defensive medicine'.

Evidence for the United States, nevertheless, indicates that doctors do respond to increasing litigation and rising court awards. A survey of 1,240 doctors by the American Medical Association found that 57 per cent of respondents claimed to be keeping better records as a result of rising costs of medical negligence. A survey of 1,646 obstetricians and gynaecologists by the American College of Obstetrics and Gynaecology in 1985 reported claims by 58.8 per cent of respondents to be monitoring patients more closely, while 44.2 per cent of the respondents said that they consulted medical colleagues more frequently over the progress of a case (Quam, 1988). Signals that can be sent via the level of indemnity insurance do not then appear to be in doubt. It is not argued here that the system in the USA has succeeded in generating an 'efficient' set of signals via indemnity insurance. However, it is argued that, where these costs have been borne by doctors, there is a response in terms of medical decision taking. It is, therefore, reasonable to ask how efficiently signals and incentives operate in the UK.

## 2.4 Incentives and Signals: A Critique of Medical Negligence Arrangements in the UK

There is a number of reasons for believing that the information flow from court damages to the decision calculus of doctors is attenuated in the UK. The effect of such attenuation is likely to reduce the significance of the marginal benefit function in Figure 2.2. Effectively it would be shifted to the left and the deterrent impact of failing to approximate reasonable standards of care would thereby be reduced. This is not to say that doctors are, in general, indifferent to the standards of care they provide. Certainly the welfare of their patient is likely to be a matter of concern to them and undoubtedly they will experience remorse should they fail to provide good professional standards of care. Any failure will reduce the doctor's prestige within his peer group and the prospect of being 'dragged' through the courts can hardly be considered as costless. It is not being argued that the marginal benefit function in Figure 2.2 loses all relevance. However, in terms of the pecuniary benefits of approximating a 'professional' standard, there is reason to doubt whether the disincentive to negligence works in exactly the way described above. The following distortions of signals which may flow between court awards and doctors' practice support this proposition.

## 2.4.1 The Pricing of Professional Indemnity Insurance

In order to prevent doctors being negligent, it has been argued that doctors should be subject to a claims-related insurance premium. Typically the structure of premiums set by medical defence societies in the UK has not been claims-related. Premiums make no allowance for the future expected costs for particular individual doctors or as between doctors in different specialities. Whilst, in aggregate, rates may be set in line with expected claims against members, they are set on a flat-rate basis, i.e. the same price for each member. Doctors in some specialities will inevitably prove more vulnerable to greater losses from negligence and, with higher damages, they might expect higher insurance premiums if insurance were provided more competitively.

In the United States, for example, the costs of insurance vary enormously as between states and medical specialism. Figures published in 1987 by the St Paul's company (a leading American medical indemnity insurer) indicate that a neurosurgeon in Chicago could expect to pay an annual premium of $192,000, whilst a physician in Houston practising no surgery and no obstetric

*Table 2.3*  SUBSCRIPTION RATES FOR THE MEDICAL DEFENCE UNION 1987 AND 1988 (INCLUDING CONCESSIONARY RATES FOR JUNIOR DOCTORS)

|  | Medical | |
|---|---|---|
|  | 1987 | 1988 |
|  | £ | £ |
| First Year | 54 | 180 |
| Second Year | 132 | 240 |
| Third Year | 210 | 396 |
| Fourth Year | 264 | 492 |
| Fifth Year | 318 | 600 |
| Sixth Year | 396 | 744 |
| Seventh Year Standard Rate | 576 | 1080 |
| Associate/non-clinical | 120 | 132 |
| Special rate for low income (earning ceiling £5,500) | 192 | — |
| Special rate for low income earners (first tier £6,230) | — | 360 |
| * Special rate for low income earners (second tier £12,460) | — | 720 |
| Doctors'/Dentists' retainer scheme | 192 | 360 |
| * HM Forces | — | 540 |

* Newly introduced rate 1988

SOURCE *Journal of the Medical Defence Union*, vol 4 (Summer 1988, p 34) procedures would be paying about $5,200 per annum. While not suggesting that such premiums are optimal, they clearly reflect more accurately the expected future losses on an individual practitioner basis.

The structure of premiums in the UK has shown a complete absence of any relation between particular premiums and claims experience or expected future losses. The pricing policy of medical defence societies has been to shoulder the responsibiliies of medical negligence *collectively* and, therefore, such variation as exists between the premiums of different doctors relates to ability to pay rather than to expected future losses of individuals. The result of this is that discounts offered are perverse. From Table 2.3 it is clear that discounts are given to those earning less and to the newer members of the profession (typically the junior hospital doctor). However, it is known that doctors in training grades (junior doctors), with less experience, constitute 30 per cent of the profession but are responsible for 40 per cent of payouts. It is possible to rationalise such a collective arrangement amongst doctors (Bowles and Jones, 1989c). Its persistence may easily be explained by the absence of competition in the provision of indemnity insurance.

With the rapid growth in the absolute value of insurance premiums, the pricing structure currently applied becomes ever more vulnerable to competition from private companies who would seek to attract the safer risk sections in the profession. It was predictable, therefore, that new schemes would be initiated to challenge the cross-subsidised rates of the medical defence societies (Bowles and Jones, 1989b). In 1988 a new scheme was introduced. The Medical Practitioners' Defence Society now offers a scheme which would offer coverage only to general practitioners. GPs suffer fewer claims than hospital doctors and have become increasingly irritated at the amount they are having to pay to 'subsidise' their hospital counterparts. The new scheme offers GPs a chance to vote with their feet and could, at the very least, be expected to put pressure on the extant defence organisations. Under the Insurance Companies Act of 1982, approval for the scheme is required from the Department of Trade and Industry.

Even more recently there has been another proposed scheme to attract the safer hospital medical specialisms. Anaesthetists and obstetricians will be less attractive to profit-making insurance companies than, for example, hospital doctors in dermatalology or geriatrics. Competition is leading to a situation where different contracts are being offered to high and low risk doctors. Such an outcome accords well with economic theory (McKenna, 1986, pp 93–8).

The thrust of competition has then finally been felt by the traditional medical defence societies. One defence society is now to offer different contracts to obstetricians, because the biggest drain on the resources has been awards to brain-damaged children (Bolt, 1989). This is a small step towards claims-related premiums and, in terms of signalling where extra medical care is most desirable, it may appear appropriate. If, as a consequence, the NHS has to pay doctors in the riskier specialisms higher salaries, then health service managers will have to consider more carefully the kind of service offered in high-risk areas of practice.

## 2.4.2 Attenuation of signals by the NHS

An improvement in the pricing of insurance premiums would only be of consequence if doctors responded to the signals that were thereby created. Will doctors respond to signals generated by the price of indemnity insurance premiums?

In the UK there is reason to doubt that, even if signals were appropriate, their impact would really be brought to bear on doctors. General practitioners' insurance premiums are a recoverable practice expense; for hospital doctors, tax relief ameliorates the burden of indemnity insurance premiums. In 1987 the Review Body on Doctors' and Dentists' Remuneration made allowance in their proposed salary increases for the fact that indemnity insurance premiums had risen sharply. In 1988 the Review Body went further and proposed that medical defence society subscriptions should be shared: one third by the doctor and two thirds by the NHS. While this ameliorates the financial burden to the doctors, there can be no such thing as a 'free lunch', for the cost will fall on the hard-pressed NHS and the taxpayer. It is important also to note that it leaves the doctor paying just one third of a subscription which is based on the *average* claims experience of the whole profession. With no individual claims-relation of subscriptions there is no direct pressure on the pocket of any unusually careless practitioner.

While the pecuniary impact of indemnity insurance premiums is undoubtedly reduced for doctors in the NHS, we have already stated that there are non-pecuniary considerations. Therefore, while the marginal benefit curve is probably shifted to the left in Figure 2.2, there is no reason to suppose that it is not relevant. In these circumstances it is impossible to deduce that the level of care is lower than the 'efficient' level. While signals work less than perfectly, there is no clear reason to believe that doctors within the National Health Service are made aware of the medical costs of additional care. It is quite possible, within this institutional arrangement, that availability rather than cost is the means by which rationing occurs. At any moment of time there may be virtually no cost charged to the practitioner for additional diagnostic tests up to capacity limits. In this case the marginal costs of additional medical care would be constant up to capacity limits and, thereafter, become vertical. The implication would be that capacity constraints to the doctor play a more relevant constraint on additional medical care than the true resource costs. Recent proposals outlined in the Government's White Paper (1989) may, of course, alter this situation as far as general practitioners are concerned. The cost to their budget of additional use of hospital facilities may become more visible.

The importance of signals and incentives is evident as far as the individual doctor is concerned. However, the information to be transmitted from the courts has, up to now, been assumed to be the 'correct' level of damages. If the courts 'under-award', then even if the signals and incentives work perfectly the individual doctor will still operate with a marginal benefit function that is 'too far' to the left. Moreover, at the same time this distortion will prove offensive to victims seeking equitable treatment. They will be 'under compensated' for the loss they have experienced. Court awards are clearly important for both efficiency and equity reasons. Moreover, if individuals feel a grievance it is important that they can present their case to the courts. To the extent that there are barriers to this process, the damages which practitioners become aware of will be lower than the true costs and also the victims will have inadequate redress for their grievance.

## 2.4.3 The Size of Court Awards

It has been argued, following Komesar and Schwartz (1978) that the value of awards should be set by courts according to the expected losses that the patient might experience as a consequence of negligence. Doctors, either explicitly or implicitly (through changes in the size of their insurance premiums) would then detect those instances in which further care is most required. At the same time, there is a moral argument claiming that it is only 'right' that those who have suffered from negligence should be compensated for their losses.

In the UK the value of awards set by courts is far removed from the recommendations of Komesar and Schwartz (1978). First, it is widely acknowledged that malpractice awards are lower in the UK than in other countries because social security and the provision of medical services at zero user cost reduce the expected private losses of victims of malpractice. It may be argued that this is reasonable, in so far as social security arrangements mitigate the harm to the victim, but in terms of efficiency it is inappropriate for it reduces the costs of negligence which are transmitted to practitioners.

Second, the general popularity of the NHS is said to keep awards lower than they would otherwise be. This may be reflected both in a disinclination to make claims and also in a willingness to settle claims for relatively modest sums.

Third, critics have argued that, in the UK, the impact of negligence upon medical practitioners is stifled because historically the judiciary has shown bias in favour of the profession when hearing malpractice suits. Miller (1986) for example notes that: 'If British doctors really have little to fear from malpractice litigation, and the evidence suggests that this is true, then a potentially effective mechanism for improving standards of care is not used to its full capacity' (p 446).

All of these arguments lead to the conclusion that the impact of medical negligence upon indemnity insurance premiums is in any event reduced and that victims in the past may have received less than fair treatment from the courts. The reverse scenario would, of course, be equally undesirable. Emotive claims about the waste of resources caused by 'defensive medicine' are often made in criticisms of the US health care system and some British doctors clearly have worries that such practices are becoming more widespread in the UK. From an economic perspective, defensive medicine is only wasteful to the extent that it involves using more resources than can be justified by the benefits which result. In such instances the signal that doctors would be receiving would be that the benefits from additional diagnostic tests etc exceeded their true value. Evidence on defensive medicine in the USA does not suggest a widespread problem. The excesses of care and treatment are often explained rather more in terms of the ability to benefit from asymmetry of information and lead patients to consume excessively. In the USA doctors paid on a fee-for-service basis clearly have an incentive to engage in needlessly elaborate tests and procedures, and it is perfectly possible that it is this pressure, rather than pressure from the courts which is the cause of the proliferation of apparently unnecessary precautionary activity. British dentists for example, who are also paid on a fee-for-services basis, have recently been criticised precisely because they have been providing unnecessary treatment.

While in this section we have argued that the judiciary should take care in setting awards, the question may be posed as to whether they should perform any role at all. The question arises as to whether the Komesar and Schwartz (1978) formula *should* be taken as an appropriate basis for the valuation of medical negligence. Some would argue that to subject doctors to signals from the courts is not just objectionable, because the signals may be distorted, but is wrong in principle. Thus a Conservative MP (Andrew Rowe, quoted in Warden, 1987) observes: 'We are allowing the courts and insurance companies an increasing say in the way doctors work, and I am not sure I want to have medical priorities dictated in that way'. This position raises the difficult question of how else one would want to have medical priorities dictated. If doctors themselves are to make the judgements without having to 'look over their shoulders' to anticipate the response of the courts to their actions then the scope for bad or careless practice becomes increasingly difficult to monitor and control. Any suggestion that there be a greater input from health service managers trained in resource allocation would almost certainly be strongly resisted by doctors who have traditionally had a high degree of autonomy and have successfully resisted threats to clinical freedom.

To leave matters completely to the profession itself would not mean that the valuation that was placed on negligence accorded with a valuation of losses to the individual concerned. Given asymmetry of information, professional bodies may well be inclined to value more highly that form of negligence which brings the profession into disrepute, by comparison with that form of negligence which actually leads the affected party to high personal losses. On this basis it is doubtful that it is sensible to leave matters in the hands of a self regulatory body. It is not sufficient to look to the General Medical Council as a satisfactory alternative mechanism for maintenance of professional standards of medical care. Indeed, it has been argued that the primary objective of the GMC is to respond to the harm that one practitioner does to the profession, rather than as an insurance mechanism to safeguard the patient. Lees (1966, p 30) notes that:

> Professional claims to be custodians of consumer welfare would cut more ice if their associations expelled members for incompetence. But they do not do so, preferring to act like any club by protecting their own. It is difficult, for example, for the plaintiff to get a doctor to testify against the defendant in cases of medical negligence.

The absence of an incentive mechanism created by experience-related insurance is then a matter of public concern: it is not sufficient to rely on the professional bodies. Klein (1973, p 170) said that 'if it is the function of the courts to deal with the doctor who damages his patient, it is the function of the General Medical Council to deal with the doctor who damages his own profession'.

Efficiency and equity both suggest a role for liability rules and the law courts. It seems appropriate that awards be guided by the principles outlined by Komesar and Scwhartz (1978). However it is important also that those individuals who are victims of negligence have access to the courts.

## 2.4.4 Access to Litigation

One of the problems associated with tort relates to the costs involved and the adversarial nature of proceedings between patient and doctor. Obviously the costs and time involved may deter victims from bringing or continuing actions. Hawkins and Paterson (1987) discovered that of 100 cases taken at random from the files of the West Midland RHA, 73 actions had been withdrawn at the end of a three year period, 14 were pending, 12 were settled out of court and one had been lost in court.

In a recent study by Bowles and Jones (1989a) it was possible to provide some indication of the length of time in dealing with cases. From the claims made at a Regional Health Authority between 1982 and 1988, it is possible in Table 2.4 to show the percentage of cases still unresolved. There remain for example eight live files relating to 36 claims initiated in 1982 and 12 live files among the 64 claims brought in 1983. Inevitably the fraction of claims resolved drops ( in row 4) as one moves on to claims brought in 1984 and falls to ten per cent for 1987. Of the claims known to have been resolved by August 1988, around 32 per cent resulted in a payment to the plaintiff. Many of the 'unresolved' claims are likely to be abandoned so that the figure of 32 per cent probably overestimates the chance of a successful result. Even so, it is broadly in line with the figure of 30–40 per cent success rate in medical cases found by the Pearson Commission ten years ago.

The poor prospect of success together with the high costs to the plaintiff of bringing an unsuccessful claim combine to operate as a major deterrent to the injured patient considering making a claim. It would be surprising if this were not having the effect of keeping some instances of medical negligence out of the public domain. In terms of the costs of litigation it is true that these may be mitigated, to some extent, by the availability of legal aid. However, there are questions as to its coverage and as to the availability of specialist legal advice which plaintiffs would require. In the USA the system of contingent fees, under which the lawyer is paid a fraction of any recovery made rather than a fixed fee, may be thought to increase the incentive for appellants to bring cases. However, this system is not as important in this respect as might at first be thought. Lawyers who share the risks with their clients are only likely to do so if they regard the risk as worth taking.

*Table 2.4*  CLAIMS FOR MEDICAL NEGLIGENCE 1982–8 IN A REGIONAL HEALTH
AUTHORITY AND THEIR OUTCOME

|  | 1982 | 1983 | 1984 | 1985 | 1986 | 1987 | 1988* | Total 82–88 |
|---|---|---|---|---|---|---|---|---|
| 1  no of claims initiated | 36 | 64 | 75 | 78 | 133 | 129 | 63 | 578 |
| 2  no of these claims resolved by August 1988 | 28 | 52 | 50 | 45 | 35 | 13 | 1 | 224 |
| 3  no of payments resulting | 12 | 16 | 18 | 12 | 10 | 4 | 0 | 72 |
| 4  % of claims resolved by August 1988 (2–1) | 77.8 | 81.3 | 66.7 | 57.8 | 26.3 | 10.1 | 1.6 | 38.8 |
| 5  % of all claims resulting in payment by August 1988 (3–1) | 33.3 | 25.0 | 24.0 | 15.4 | 7.5 | 3.1 | — | 12.5 |
| 6  % of resolved claims involving payment (3–2) | 42.9 | 30.8 | 36.0 | 26.7 | 28.6 | 30.8 | — | 32.1 |

*  Up to August 1988

SOURCE  Bowles and Jones (1989a)

## 2.5  Compensating and Loss-spreading

From what we have just said about access to litigation it follows that injured patients differ in their capacity to press claims. Low income patients may obtain legal aid and high income patients may be able to finance their own legal action privately. But for the large number of people in the middle income bracket litigation may look like an unaffordable luxury. A system offering more equal access would look more attractive.

Another criticism of negligence, and one of the arguments for moving to a no-fault system is that patients have to wait at present a long time before they receive compensation. A no-fault scheme would enable cases to be resolved more quickly because the issue of negligence is set aside. It should also be less expensive to use and thus more patients would be in a position to recover some of their losses. While these arguments suggest that a system of no-fault would be more equitable, it is important to note that the advocates of no-fault expect that the greater number of claims made would cause a strain on resources, and individual awards would have to be restricted to much lower levels than a court would consider appropriate. This raises the normative issue of whether it is preferable for victims of serious negligence to secure full compensation or whether it is more important to provide a lower level of redress more generally across the board.

The other key weakness of a negligence rule in this area is that patients suffering similar injuries from treatment may be dealt with differently. The trigger for compensation is the lack of reasonable care rather than the injury *per se*.

## 2.6   Costs of Administration and Legal Expenses; Transaction Costs of Medical Negligence in the UK

A frequent criticism of the tort system is the very high cost of its administration relative to the sums paid to successful litigants. Adverse comparisons with the costs of administering the social security system have been one of the arguments used in favour of a no-fault or strict liability approach to medical injury. The recent Civil Justice Review study, for example, put the total costs of a High Court action at 50–70 per cent of damages recovered. Some years previously the Pearson Commission (1978) had estimated the administrative costs of tort at 85 per cent of damages, the comparable figure for social security payments being 11 per cent. These figures have to be treated with considerable care, because, of course, a no-fault approach would still involve questions as to exactly what classes of contingencies are to be covered. Injuries which are an unavoidable consequence of treatment and injuries which could have been avoided by following a different but inadvisable medical procedure constitute just two of the grey areas in which there would almost certainly persist some uncertainty and some need for costly determinations as to whether the insurance fund is liable to pay compensation.

An indication of the administrative costs of the present arrangements for professional liability in the medical field (based on the accounts of the Medical Defence Union) has been provided in Bowles and Jones (1988). Using the Pearson Commission approach, it is possible to make an estimate of the ratio of administrative costs to payments of damages. If it is assumed that expenditure by plaintiffs on lawyers matches expenditure by the MDU, a conservative estimate of the ratio of legal costs to recoveries can be provided. Estimates based on this principle (A) are shown for 1986–8 in Table 2.5. It is clear that legal costs may exceed the value of the award. However, an alternative approach would be to compare estimated recoveries, as already defined, net of imputed legal cost indemnities for plaintiffs, with *total* administrative costs fo the MDU, i.e. including the provision of advisory services. Estimated on this principle (B) the costs of administration and legal expenses rises substantially.

It has been estimated that a statutory strict-liability insurance based scheme would cost around £50 million (Warden, 1987). If this total is split between administrative costs and payments to plaintiffs at the average social security ratio of 11:100, this would give compensation payments of around £45 million and costs of £5 million. Of course, a strict liability scheme could take many forms and its total cost may vary by a large amount depending on decisions on issues such as the ceiling set on compensation levels and the complexity and stringency of the test to determine whether a claim will be met. The general presumption would be that such a scheme would be likely to raise significantly the numbers receiving compensation, but to reduce the average amount recovered. However, on the estimates made above there is every reason to believe that, by comparison to tort, no-fault might be cheaper to administer in both absolute and relative terms.

*Table 2.5*  ADMINISTRATIVE AND LEGAL COSTS IN RELATION TO AWARDS OF
DAMAGES

|   |   | £ million | | |
|---|---|---|---|---|
|   |   | 1985 | 1986 | 1987 |
| 1 | Indemnity payments | 11.5 | 14.8 | 17.4 |
| 2 | Legal costs (insurer's) | 4.2 | 4.3 | 5.4 |
| 3 | Administrative costs | 1.9 | 2.1 | 2.6 |
| 4 | Damages payments (row 1 minus row 2) | 7.3 | 10.5 | 12.0 |
| 5 | Estimated legal costs (both sides, row 2 × 2) | 8.4 | 8.6 | 10.8 |
| 6 | Principle A: Ratio of estimated legal costs to awards of damages (row 5/row 4) | 1.13 | 0.81 | 0.90 |
| 7 | Principle B: Ratio of total administrative costs to awards of damages ((row 3 + row 5)/row 4) | 1.38 | 1.01 | 1.12 |

NOTE    Ratios calculated from non-rounded data
SOURCE  Medical Defence Union Accounts, *MDU Annual Reports* 1986–8


## 2.7  Conclusions and Summary

In this chapter we have sought to apply the theoretical analysis discussed in
Chapter one. The framework of Calabresi (1970) focuses attention on
efficiency, equity and the transactions costs implied by a negligence procedure.
We can conclude briefly that:

> on efficiency criteria several reasons explain why doctors will not be subject to the
> full pecuniary costs of medical negligence and why, therefore, 'inefficiency' may
> ensue;

> as regards equity, the negligence rule is one whereby victims generally have received
> less than adequate recompense, and then only after incurring substantial delay;

> the administrative and litigation costs of the current system are substantial and this
> may well prove a barrier to patients who have grievances.

There is no question but that there is room for reform of the tort system and
this is a theme to which we return in the conclusions of this study. With respect
to access to litigation, there is much to be said for those recommendations
made in a recent study by the King's Fund (1988). For example: legal aid might
be made easier, contingency fee litigation might be permitted (as the Lord
Chancellor has recently proposed); fee splitting arrangements between solicitors and more specialist firms might be introduced and greater information
about legal services and the special skills of solicitors could be made available
to plaintiffs.

However, at this stage, we would resist the conclusion that the current system is in need of replacement by a system of no-fault. To make such a recommendation requires far closer scrutiny of the implications of the precise details of any particular no-fault scheme. More generally our concern would be that, whatever the merits of such a scheme in terms of administrative costs, there are reasons for concern about it on both equity and efficiency grounds.

Under present arrangements victims who have a case of negligence will not bring the case because of the costs and the uncertainty involved. The counter argument is that, other things equal, the greater the injustice and the more obvious the negligence, the less likely is there to be a barrier. In the first instance there would clearly have to be adequate safeguards under no-fault that compensation to plaintiffs, particularly those suffering the greatest loss, was not artificially limited by the constraints of budgets in order to satisfy in full the disputes of those whose losses had not been as great or as obvious.

While we recognise that under the negligence system the link between court damages and pecuniary sanction on doctors is weak, we would be concerned that under no-fault the deterrent role of sanction may be weakened even further. It is a matter of some concern that in those examples where no fault arrangements have already been instituted the number of accidents, other things equal, has increased (Landes, 1982). Under the tort system doctors who are negligent will find no pleasure in the recognition of this within the law courts, but how will monitoring and sanctions be enforced with no-fault? Without adequate safeguards the marginal benefits of higher standards of professionalism (as represented in Figure 2.2) will be weakened further. If accidents were to increase the alleged saving in transactions costs would be called in question.

Pressure is clearly building up for greater government involvement in the provision of no-fault. If it is to be the case that the NHS takes a more active role in indemnifying doctors, then we have proposed (Bowles and Jones 1989b) that the Department of Health might institute a scheme which refunds a doctor in any speciality for the basic indemnity insurance premium but they would not refund any loading which might be justified as a result of a poor claims record. This would be one method to retain a sanction and incentive for doctors to emulate the standards of care which might reasonably be expected within their peer group.

## NOTES

1 Danzon (1985) illustrates this by way of the following example. An individual faces a probability of 1 in 100 of a theft of goods valued at £1,000 but, if he bought a lock, the probability of theft would fall to 1 in 1,000. The expected gain from purchase of the lock is the reduction in the probability of theft multiplied by the size of the loss £9. If the lock costs less than £9 he should purchase the lock but moral hazard suggests that with insurance he will not. If premiums were set so that he paid £10 without a lock and £1 with a lock, the problem of moral hazard would be resolved. The solution lies in utilising sufficient information to set premiums to reflect expected future losses. If doctors signal, by their claims record, that they are likely to be 'bad risks' in the future then they will expect, on this analysis, to incur higher insurance premiums. In this way the insurance premium creates an incentive mechanism for doctors to take reasonable care in their professional practice.

# 3   The Legal Profession

## 3.1   Introduction

Lawyers, like other professionals, can and do make mistakes. The consequences of their errors or omissions will often be less readily discernible than those of the medical practitioners we looked at in the previous chapter. The amounts at stake can be much larger however, since large-scale commercial operations in which lawyers are involved may amount to hundreds of millions of pounds. With even small errors being potentially very costly, high professional standards are demanded, and this makes actions for professional negligence potentially a very powerful threat.

The legal profession in England has long been divided into two parts. Barristers are small in number and heavily concentrated in London and to a lesser extent other large provincial cities. They act as advocates in the higher courts, write opinions on cases and exercise other specialist functions. There is no negligence action available in respect of advocacy although barristers can be sued for negligence in the giving of advice.

Solicitors by contrast are numerous and widespread. They do a wider range of work and can be sued for negligence. The ending in the 1980s of the monopoly of conveyancing which solicitors had for long enjoyed has helped to accelerate the trend towards larger firms and greater specialisation. At least for the moment, the high street solicitor remains the legal profession's counterpart to the General Practitioner in medicine.

Following publication in January 1989 of three Green Papers by the Lord Chancellor's Department for a major overhaul of the structure of the legal profession, a dismantling of many of the barriers which currently prevent solicitors from appearing as advocates in the higher courts and of the barriers preventing estate agents and mortgage lenders from offering conveyancing services is contemplated. The future evolution of the legal profession is thus subject to considerable uncertainty. We concentrate in this chapter on solicitors because they constitute the bulk of the profession. The arguments and analysis applying to barristers are fundamentally similar.

The very large size of potential claims against firms of solicitors has the effect of making it virtually imperative for them to carry indemnity insurance. Most firms of solicitors are organised as partnerships, each partner being liable personally for the firm's debts and thus, in effect, responsible for the actions of his fellow-partners. The prospect of personal bankruptcy is quite sufficient to induce solicitors to indemnify themselves against large claims which would immediately bankrupt all partners in the firm.

## 3.2 Solicitors and Indemnity Insurance

The observation that solicitors for the most part considered it prudent to take out indemnity insurance, and that the confidence of prospective clients might thereby be improved, led the Law Society in the late 1970s to introduce a compulsory indemnity insurance scheme for its members. This arrangement has the advantage for solicitors of providing the Law Society with a high degree of monopsony power in the insurance market. Better terms are available to a single large buyer than to a large number of small buyers. By shopping around and wielding their market power the Law Society have been able to attract competitive quotations and thus to keep premiums below the levels to which they might otherwise have risen. As we shall see later, the Law Society have recently gone one stage further and now, in effect, run their own insurance fund.

It is standard practice for solicitors to buy 'top-up' indemnity insurance on the commercial market to complement the fixed-limit, compulsory cover (discussed in more detail below) provided through the Law Society scheme. This 'top-up' market operates along conventional commercial indemnity insurance lines. The practice gets a quotation from one or more of the brokers specialising in this area by filling in a proposal form which asks for details of the kind of work the firm does, its gross fee income and the number of claims it has made under previous policies.

To some degree the thoroughness of this indemnity insurance may have the conventional 'moral hazard' effect (outlined in Chapter 1) of isolating the practitioner's pocket from any carelessness in his own behaviour, thereby making it rather more likely that accidents will happen. Insurance companies, well aware of the consequences of compounding risks in this way, have developed a number of techniques for minimising such problems. Screening practitioners so as to identify high risk individuals who are charged correspondingly higher premiums is one method and the Law Society's own compulsory scheme has such a safeguard built into it.

'Loading' the premiums of firms with bad claims experience has pretty much the same effect as the 'no claims bonus' familiar to the motorist. The careful (and, it must be said, the lucky) pay smaller premiums than those making heavy claims. Sooner or later, of course, the lucky but careless motorist is likely to have an accident just as the careless solicitor is likely to be sued successfully for damages for professional negligence.

According to the analysis in Chapter 1 of the practitioner's choice of level of care, premium loading is likely to mean that the lawyer confronts what might be termed a 'costs of insurance' schedule which indicates that failure to exercise a reasonable degree of care will be costly for him. If his work is always up to standard the practitioner will not be sued successfully for negligence, and his premium will reflect the fact. The more often the level of care falls below the

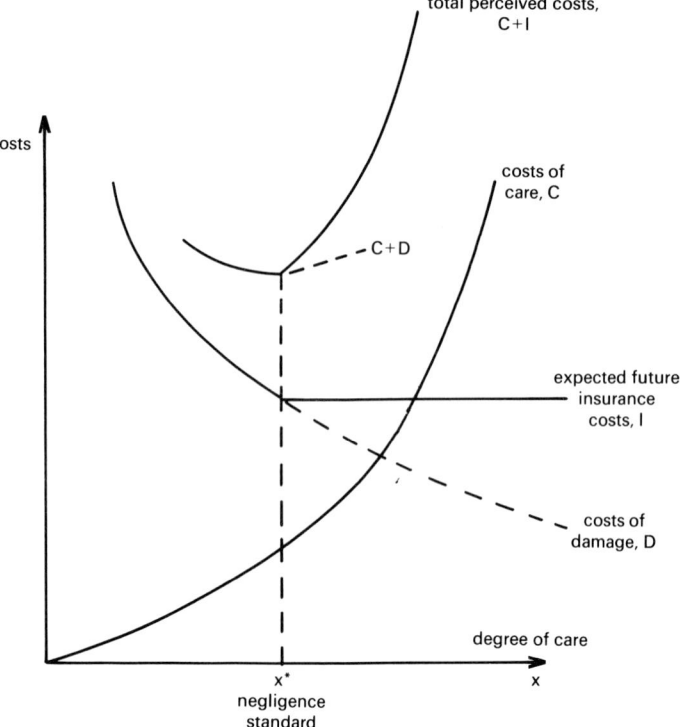

Figure 3.1   Insurance and the choice of level of care

level judged to be reasonable the more frequently the lawyer will be found liable, and the higher will be the premium he has to pay for insurance.

We can represent this as in Figure 3.1 with a cost of insurance schedule (I) replacing the cost of harm schedule of Chapter 1. For simplicity we assume that, until the degree of care drops below the level at which liability will be found under a negligence rule, insurance costs are constant. It will generally be difficult (and rarely profitable) for insurers to monitor care above the reasonable care standard, with the result that particularly careful practitioners will not be offered special discounts. Below the efficient level of care, x*, we characterise premiums as rising steadily in line with the increase in expected damage costs. In practice, as we will see, premiums tend to rise in steps. Further, the insurer will find it difficult to ensure a perfect match between premiums and the expected cost of meeting claims. But the insurer does have an incentive to keep the two in line so as to avoid the adverse selection problem. If he offers relatively attractive terms to poor risks he will find such risks over-represented in his portfolio and as a company will lose money heavily.

In drawing the diagram we incorporate both the expected insurance costs and the costs of harm schedule familiar from Chapter 1. The purpose of including the latter is to emphasise our assumption that, in deciding whether the lawyer is liable, the court will apply a standard of care x* which sets the marginal cost of care equal to the marginal cost of the damage resulting. With this standard in place, the lawyer allowing his standards to drop below x* can expect to pay higher premiums in the future, but on our assumption that the premium paid by the practitioner reflects the degree of risk he represents, the cost of insurance schedule will have the same shape as the cost of damage schedule. The insurance schedule is shown above the cost of damage schedule because there will be costs involved in administering the insurance.

Under the negligence rule which applies to the legal practitioner the diagram indicates that the lawyer has an incentive, even with indemnity insurance cover, to choose the efficient degree of care. The total costs as perceived by the lawyer are the sum of the expected insurance cost schedule and the cost of care schedule. The minimum point on this schedule occurs at the level of care x* which corresponds with the level a court would consider reasonable, suggesting that a negligence rule is consistent with efficiency.

As will become evident in this chapter and the next, the claims record of an individual practitioner or practice is a basic piece of information required by underwriters offering professional indemnity insurance in all areas other than medicine. The notion of 'collective responsibility' which is now coming under pressure as competitive forces enter the medical negligence sphere is conspicuous by its absence from almost all other professions. The Law Society's compulsory scheme, as we shall see, loads the solicitors' premiums in proportion to the amount paid by way of claims under the policy.

In addition to screening those seeking insurance, insurers use other devices familiar from elsewhere in the insurance market to encourage the practitioner to exercise appropriate levels of care. Deductibles, under which the practitioner pays the first £x of any claim are one obvious way of discouraging carelessness, since they maintain a direct, albeit limited, sanction on the lawyer against whom successful claims are made. An 'excess' of this kind may well have the added advantage for the insurer of reducing the number of small claims he has to meet. As well as helping to control the overall cost of claims this eases the administrative burden of investigating small claims which are likely to be disproportionately costly to handle.

## 3.3 The Role of Reputation

The legal profession in the UK, unlike the great majority of the medical profession, provide services almost exclusively through markets. This mode of service delivery provides a second means through which law firms are encouraged to act carefully. The law firm's reputation will be one of the influences on its success. If it comes to be known as a firm which offers variable (or consistently low) service quality it can expect to lose clients and to be forced to lower its fees relative to other competing firms.

Prospective clients of a firm might be deterred if they discover that a firm is frequently being sued for negligence. At the same time, a reputation for uniformly high quality service should have a positive effect making it easier for the firm to attract new clients and enabling the firm to charge higher fees. The effectiveness with which the firm can market a superior reputation will depend of course on the ease with which the firm can advertise and the extent to which it is allowed by the regulatory agency responsible for the profession to make claims about being superior to other firms. The traditional, rather negative, approach to such matters has had the effect of limiting the information that firms of solicitors are allowed to publicise about their record. The effect of such limitation tends to be that only bad reputations receive public attention. The scandalously inept advice or whatever that attracts media coverage may hit a firm hard but any corresponding good news that a firm is acting particularly sensibly or carefully does not.

Despite the pressures for firms of solicitors to exercise high levels of competence and care, there are certain facts about legal services which may inhibit the effectiveness of the quality control which market reputation and the indemity insurance arrangements exercise together. The central problems are very much the standard ones outlined in Chapter 1. First, there is the asymmetry of information. You engage a solicitor to give you advice, to carry out transactions (or whatever) on your behalf precisely because you very often do not know what needs to be done or how to do it.

Having once employed a lawyer you are in the position of having to rely on him or her to make sensible judgements and to take appropriate steps on your behalf. Not knowing what these steps might be or what might comprise a sensible judgement often makes it difficult to assess the quality of service received even after the event. A poorly drafted will which fails to give rise to the disposition of estate as you intended may be a rather extreme example.

Another example is provided by a recent case in which an injured patient finally succeeded in recovering a large sum of damages for medical negligence. Before the award was finally made the plaintiff had received advice from solicitors to accept the offer of an out-of-court settlement which represented only a tiny fraction of the sum finally recovered by the very determined persons pressing his claim. At the time of making the initial recommendation to settle, the solicitors did not have a complete picture of the course of events leading up to the incident in question. In recommending acceptance they were (we presume) making informed guesses about the likely content of further enquiries and weighing the value of these enquiries against the additional costs the plaintiff would face in terms of fees and costs. With the benefit of hindsight one can see that they were mistaken in their belief that further evidence and enquiry were not worth the cost. But this is not sufficient to prove that they were negligent: that would require a demonstration that they had not exercised a reasonable degree of care.

This case came to light only because those acting for the plaintiff opted to ignore the professional advice and to seek a second opinion. Such decisions are risky and costly and therefore will not be taken very often. The likelihood that advice from a second professional will be different is relatively small if the standard of service is fairly homogeneous across professionals. The client has to have a considerable amount at stake before considering such a step. This is likely to mean that many clients never really know whether they have received good advice or bad. They may know that the solicitor takes a pessimistic view of the likely outcome of a court hearing, but only rarely will the reliability of the view be tested.

Two important conclusions can be derived from this example. First, solicitors are in a relatively powerful position in relation to clients and the chances of the solicitor being found to have given negligent advice are relatively small. Secondly, clients know *before* they visit a lawyer that they *may* receive bad advice. The prudent client is likely therefore to exercise care in his choice of practitioner.

In the case of solicitors the professional's reputation may play a central role in the control of quality of service. The plaintiff will be very unlikely to go back to a solicitor from whom he suspects he has had bad service. Equally, he is very unlikely to say a good word for the solicitor when talking to friends, relatives or colleagues. In addition to the risk of bad 'word of mouth' publicity the solicitor who may be prone to carelessness has to take account also of the prospect of mistakes receiving media coverage. Extensive damage and loss of confidence may therefore result from what, on the face of the matter, seems a rather trifling error.

It is interesting in the light of this argument to reconsider the position of the barrister. A poor court performance does not leave the barrister open to a claim from his client but it may well persuade the solicitor retaining the barrister's services to take his next case to a different barrister. Since barristers' services have to be enlisted via solicitors, it is reasonable to suppose that the demand for barristers is well informed, so that reputational concerns exercise a strong influence on the quality of barristers' work. The additional element of quality control which a negligence action would permit may thus be rather limited and difficult to justify.

### 3.4 The Law Society's Indemnity Insurance Scheme

From August 1976 it became compulsory, under the Solicitor's Indemnity Rules, for every practising solicitor in England and Wales to effect indemnity cover under the Law Society's Master Policy. The rationale for moving away from the earlier non-regulated position, in which it was open to solicitors to make their own indemnity insurance arrangements, was a financial one. By insuring collectively, the hope was that the profession could get much better terms from the insurance market, enabling premiums to be reduced.

Whatever the success or otherwise of the profession in achieving this objective, the scheme is of interest here because in the discussions which took place on how best to modify the scheme after its original introduction a considerable amount of information about its operation was made public. The usual difficulties surrounding efforts to acquire data on insurance market operations are thus absent for the period 1975-9, at least as far as solicitors are concerned. Although the data on the number of claims and so on are nearly a decade out of date, we can derive considerable insight into the operation of an indemnity insurance scheme.

The scheme itself can be outlined as follows. First the unit insured is the individual practitioner rather than the law firm. Secondly, the cover provided was limited to £50,000 for every sole practitioner and £30,000 per partner in larger firms. This cover was for each and every claim, irrespective of the number of claims against the firm in any given insurance year. There was however an 'excess' per claim of £400 multiplied by the number of partners. This excess, along with cover for claims in excess of the firm's maximum cover under the Master Scheme, could be insured privately by the solicitor. To this extent the scheme has changed relatively little subsequently. The annual premium charged in 1979 for the scheme's coverage was £926 for Inner London practitioners and £712 for those practising elsewhere. Partners belonging to firms with a bad claims record however would face a loading of up to 50 per cent on their premium.

The way in which the loading was calculated is as follows. Where the claims paid in respect of a practice over a three-year period exceeded the total premiums paid by partners in the firm over those same three years, the partners would be charged a loading on the premium. If claims paid were between 100 per cent and 200 per cent of the premiums paid, the loading was 20 per cent. The loading then rose in steps to 30 per cent, 40 per cent and finally 50 per cent for practices making claims in excess of 400 per cent of premiums paid.

To give an example, let us assume that the premium remained constant for a provincial firm at £712 for three years. With three partners the practice would have paid premiums of $(3 \times 3 \times 712)$ over the period, namely £6,408. If it had made claims against the scheme over the same period of, say, 250 per cent of that amount (i.e. £16,020) then for the following year the partners would each face a 30 per cent loading of their premium. Each would therefore have been charged a premium of £712 plus 30 per cent, i.e. £925.60. In reality of course the basic premium will generally rise from year to year with inflation.

### 3.4.1  An analysis of claims under the Law Society's Indemnity Insurance Scheme

Information about the premium structure of the scheme gives some clues as to the relative riskiness of different groups of practitioners, but since the scheme is compulsory one cannot be sure that it is a completely reliable guide. Without being able to establish whether there is any element of cross-subsidisation between groups, it is not possible to treat the premium structure as a measure of risk. Fortunately, there are data available on claims made under the scheme over the period 1976–9 and, although this information is somewhat out-of-date, it is readily accessible and illustrates our points clearly.

Our basic premise is that the greater the degree of care the solicitor exercises, the less likely that successful claims will be made against him. Thus by examining the structure of claims it should be possible to say something about the degree of care solicitors are exercising. Our underlying hypothesis is that solicitors, as rational profit-maximising economic agents, will exercise the 'cost-justified' degree of care in their professional activities. They will choose a style of work which balances the marginal cost of additional care against the additional revenue the extra care will generate. Carelessness resulting in successful claims against the law firm may harm it in two ways. First, it may raise the firm's costs and thus depresss the incomes of partners and secondly it may damage the firm's reputation in the marketplace, with the same effect of depressing earnings.

The key determinant of the degree of care, on this approach, becomes the sensitivity of prospective consumers of a solicitor's service to his 'accident record'. As will become clear, indemnity insurance premiums account for a relatively modest fraction of solicitors' fees. With a comparatively low degree of premium loading for those with bad claims experience, it is implausible that the increase in insurance premiums *per se* can be acting as a major deterrent to carelessness. This means that the effect on market reputation is likely to be the principal disincentive to poor quality service.

Before exploring data which may help establish whether firms offering higher quality and more careful work are able to exploit their superiority through higher fees, we consider briefly the market for the services of solicitors in the UK. Over the past twenty years there have been major changes in the size distribution of firms and in the composition of their workloads. The operation of professional liability in this market cannot be properly understood without some background knowledge of this structural change.

The first, rather obvious, observation is that small, provincial firms of solicitors handle different sorts of workloads from their larger counterparts in the City of London. The smaller provincial solicitor has traditionally been more dependent on private householders and small businesses whilst the City firm relies more on large businesses. The different client base is associated with a corresponding variation both in the kind of work done and the level of fees charged. Table 3.1 illustrates the degree of variation which existed in 1975–6 in the composition of the workload of firms of different sizes. It shows that conveyancing, although relatively less important to the larger firms, was still a considerable source of revenue.

Conveyancing was traditionally a major source of profits for lawyers although it had for some time been shrinking. For example, whilst Table 3.1 shows it accounting for 47.4 per cent of all revenue in 1975–6 the corresponding figure reported by the Prices and Incomes Board in their investigation of the remuneration of solicitors (Prices and Incomes Board, 1968) a decade earlier was 55.6 per cent of income. Even in periods when the scale of charges was not laid down in relation to property value by the Law Society, the market operated as a fairly effective cartel. As recently as ten years ago it was very difficult to 'shop around' firms of solicitors in search of a competitive quotation for a straightforward domestic conveyancing transaction.

In the early 1980s the property market was relatively depressed and this, combined with pressure for increased competitiveness and legislative moves to discontinue the solicitors' monopoly of conveyancing, left many small firms struggling. The very rapid growth of property values in the mid 1980s and the expansion of the economy, particularly in the services sector, meant profitable times returned. The size composition of firms had however changed markedly. As Table 3.2 illustrates the number of sole practitioners declined over the period 1983–6, whilst the number of firms with more than ten partners had

*Table 3.1*   PERCENTAGE OF GROSS FEE INCOME FROM DIFFERENT CATEGORIES
OF WORK BY SIZE OF FIRM

| | Average gross fee income per firm | Proportion of total gross fee income 1975/76 | | | | | |
|---|---|---|---|---|---|---|---|
| | | all firms | sole practi- tioners | 2 partners | 3–4 partners | 5–9 partners | 10 or more partners |
| | £ | % | % | % | % | % | % |
| Conveyancing | 46,674 | 47.4 | 59.9 | 56.2 | 53.2 | 47.8 | 32.4 |
| Probate | 13,331 | 13.5 | 12.7 | 14.2 | 15.0 | 14.8 | 10.5 |
| Company | 12,288 | 12.5 | 3.7 | 3.8 | 5.3 | 7.8 | 32.2 |
| Other non-contentious | 4,267 | 4.3 | 3.2 | 4.9 | 3.7 | 4.6 | 4.7 |
| Matrimonial | 5,357 | 5.4 | 6.3 | 6.6 | 6.3 | 5.8 | 3.3 |
| Crime | 4,392 | 4.5 | 6.4 | 5.5 | 5.6 | 4.9 | 1.5 |
| Personal injury | 3,239 | 3.3 | 3.4 | 2.5 | 3.3 | 4.6 | 2.2 |
| Other contentious | 8,971 | 9.1 | 4.4 | 6.3 | 7.6 | 9.7 | 13.2 |
| All categories of work | 98,519 | 100.0 | 100.0 | 100.0 | 100.0 | 100.0 | 100.0 |

SOURCE   Table 16.49 in *Royal Commission on Legal Services* (London, HMSO, Cmnd 7648, vol II, 1979)

*Table 3.2*   NUMBERS OF FIRMS BY SIZE

| Size of firm | Number of firms | | | |
|---|---|---|---|---|
| number of principals | (NBPI) 1969 | Jan 1977 | Dec 1983 | Feb 1986 |
| sole practitioner | 2,640 | 2,054 | 2,809 | 2,617 |
| 2 | 1,950 | 1,699 | 1,774 | 1,802 |
| 3 | 1,350 | 932 | 1,001 | 1,087 |
| 4 | | 603 | 624 | 698 |
| 5 | | 352 | 396 | 437 |
| 6 | | 217 | 212 | 250 |
| 7 | | 148 | 172 | 196 |
| 8 | 640 | 107 | 111 | 139 |
| 9 | | 73 | 66 | 60 |
| 10 | | 50 | 75 | 85 |
| 11–15 | | 128 | 158 | 182 |
| 16–19 | | 32 | 39 | 68 |
| 20 and over | | 25 | 55 | 63 |
| | 6,580 | 6,420 | 7,492 | 7,684 |

SOURCES   Column 1, National Board for Prices and Incomes *Report on Solicitors' Remuneration, 1969*. All other data from the Law Society's *Statistical Bulletin*, 1984 and 1986 editions increased by more than 20 per cent. The number of firms in total had increased slightly but the average firm was now considerably larger than it had been.

The changing workload meant that commercial concerns increased in importance as clients. Whilst this had given impetus to the expansion of larger firms it has other implications for firms of solicitors. The large corporations upon whom the major practices rely by and large have complex and demanding requirements: they expect to pay more for legal services but do not expect mistakes to be made. They will therefore be concerned to choose their firm of solicitors with more care than the average private seller of a house. The firm's reputation is thus at a greater premium in the better-informed, higher fee end of the market. Any serious errors may result in the loss of major clients upon whom the practice relies heavily, and in 'knock-on effects' if other clients lose confidence as a result.

Information about negligence claims against solicitors will contain some clues as to whether larger practices are really, as we would conjecture, more careful and more zealous in protecting their reputation. Care has to be taken however because the practices who are taking more care will tend to charge higher prices, so that any errors they do make will generally result in higher valued claims against them. In what follows we take account of this by measuring the size of successful negligence claims in relation to the size of fees charged, therefore making an allowance for the fact that the same kind of mistake may be much more costly to the client if a large issue is at stake than if less is involved.

For example, consider a case heard in 1975 which involved a dispute about the appropriate fee for conveyancing a property valued at £2.25 million. It was agreed that thirty hours had been spent on the conveyancing. The firm's normal charge rate at that time was £15 per hour, suggesting an overall fee of around £450. In the event the hourly rate had been multiplied up to such an extent that an amount of £5,500 was allowed, implying an hourly rate of well over £300. Much of this uprating was related to the value of the property. The differential between the two rates is enormous and difficult to justify, but in principle one might expect the lawyer spending time on a major commercial transaction of this kind to be concentrating harder during the time he is at work.

From a liability perspective the solicitor is likely to be much more exposed on a high valued transaction since a mistake which gives rise, for example, to a delay in the completion of the transaction will involve greater loss to the client. If interest rates are around 1 per cent per month, as they are at the time of writing, a month's delay in receiving £2.25 million would cost the client £2,250 in lost interest, an amount he would surely expect to recover if a consequence of the solicitor's error. The practice handling a lot of high-valued transactions may not be any more error-prone than a practice dealing with small transactions but the losses it causes, and thus its insurance premiums, will be greater.

To the extent that the client can be sure that the solicitor is properly insured and that damages recoverable in the event of loss will provide adequate compensation, it could be argued that he will be indifferent as to whether the solicitor has a good reputation or not. If the market is competitive, the premium the client can expect to pay on a high-valued property would reflect purely the marginal cost of the additional liability insurance costs to the solicitor taking the job. In practice, the likelihood is that damages awarded for negligence will not fully compensate the client for the loss he suffers. The business client in particular would have to spend time, with a high opportunity cost, identifying errors which form the basis of a claim. The business will thus search for a firm of reliable solicitors so as to mitigate the expected frequency and thus costs of any such events.

In compiling the data to explore the hypothesis that commercial practices doing high-valued work stand to make more costly mistakes, we run into the 'long-tail' problem of professional liability insurance. The 'long tail' means that there are many circumstances, particularly those involving high-valued transactions, in which a long time lag intervenes between an event triggering a claim and the claim being resolved. Tables 3.3 and 3.4, contain information about claims arising during the period 1976-9, with Table 3.3 giving a break-down of payments made on these claims up to 1979 and Table 3.4 giving a breakdown of payments made *on the same set of claims* by 1982.

*Table 3.3*  CLAIMS ARISING FROM THE PERIOD 1976-9 WHICH HAD BEEN PAID BY MARCH 1979

| No of principals in firm | No of firms at April 1979 | Percentage of all principals | No of cases where payment made | Total payments made in respect of claims £ | Percentage of total amount paid | Average size of Claim £ |
|---|---|---|---|---|---|---|
| 1 | 2,285 | 11 | 206 | 848,430 | 18 | 4,119 |
| 2 | 1,608 | 16 | 214 | 651,475 | 13 | 3,044 |
| 3 | 994 | 14 | 157 | 919,253 | 19 | 5,855 |
| 4 | 581 | 11 | 126 | 498,851 | 10 | 3,959 |
| 5 | 393 | 10 | 106 | 393,662 | 8 | 3,713 |
| 6 | 223 | 7 | 52 | 207,141 | 4 | 3,983 |
| 7 | 136 | 4 | 37 | 79,607 | 2 | 2,151 |
| 8 | 101 | 4 | 27 | 277,926 | 6 | 10,293 |
| 9 | 89 | 4 | 22 | 70,100 | 1 | 3,186 |
| 10 | 62 | 3 | 27 | 121,228 | 2 | 4,489 |
| 11/15 | 131 | 8 | 48 | 470,952 | 10 | 9,811 |
| 16/20 | 32 | 3 | 11 | 76,172 | 2 | 6,924 |
| 21 and over | 32 | 5 | 17 | 226,696 | 5 | 13,335 |
| | 6,667 | 100 | 1,050 | 4,841,493 | 100 | |

Total number of principals—20,404
* The date used for the purpose of calculating experience rating.

SOURCE Table 2 in *The Future of the Indemnity Insurance Scheme* (London, Law Society, November 1979)

*Table 3.4*   CLAIMS ARISING FROM THE PERIOD 1976–9 WHICH HAD BEEN PAID BY JUNE 1982

| No of principals in firm | % of overall premium paid | No of payments made | Total payments made | % of total paid | No of total losses paid | Average size of claim |
|---|---|---|---|---|---|---|
| 1 | 12 | 436 | 2982537 | 16 | 7 | 6840 |
| 2 | 15 | 372 | 2471261 | 13 | 3 | 6643 |
| 3 | 13 | 403 | 2340455 | 13 | 0 | 5807 |
| 4 | 11 | 218 | 1619395 | 9 | 0 | 7428 |
| 5 | 9 | 140 | 1076949 | 6 | 0 | 7692 |
| 6 | 6 | 90 | 1034965 | 6 | 1 | 10454 |
| 7 | 4 | 75 | 896054 | 5 | 1 | 11947 |
| 8 | 4 | 67 | 972417 | 5 | 1 | 14513 |
| 9 | 4 | 37 | 520354 | 3 | 0 | 14063 |
| 10 | 3 | 37 | 597001 | 3 | 0 | 16135 |
| 11/15 | 8 | 88 | 1231468 | 7 | 0 | 13994 |
| 16/20 | 3 | 36 | 575441 | 3 | 0 | 16924 |
| Over 20 | 8 | 24 | 2087412 | 11 | 1 | 86975 |
| | 100 | 2032 | 18405712 | 100 | 14 | |

SOURCE *Consultative Document on the Future Basis of Premium Assessment,* Table 2 (London, Law Society, November 1982)

It can be seen that between 1976 and 1979, 1,050 claims were resolved at a cost to the insurers of £4.84 million, and thus an average cost per claim of around £4,600. This compares with a further 982 claims resolved at a cost of £13.57 million over the period from 1979 to 1982, i.e. an average per claim of nearly £14,000. Larger claims, as one might expect, are settled less quickly. Table 3.5 shows reserves, as at June 1982, in respect of 939 claims outstanding from the period 1976–9, at £24.47 million, representing an average per claim of slightly over £26,000.

This suggests that many claims (possibly more than 50 per cent) had not been resolved within three years of their having been filed. As a result of these time lags it is important to leave as long a time as possible before commenting on the composition of claims resulting from a particular time period. The long tail is of course a fairly severe problem for the insurer, especially if the rate at which claims are made (or their size) happens to be expanding rapidly. It becomes difficult to quantify potential losses on the strength of past losses, so that the insurer becomes more exposed than he may judge acceptable. It is no surprise to learn that the professional liability insurance market has experienced a degree of instability. Insurers are lured into the market by the prospect of high, profitable premiums one year only to find that they soon want to leave the market as claims build up at a rate which eats away all the expected profits.

Returning to Table 3.3 (which covers claims under the Law Society's Scheme up to 1979) the average size of claim documented in the final column suggests

*Table 3.5*   BREAKDOWN OF RESERVES AT 1.6.82 FOR INSURANCE YEARS
1.9.76–31.8.79 BY REFERENCE TO SIZE OF FIRM

| No of principals in firm | % of overall premium | No of reserves | Amount of areserves | % of reserves | No of total loss reserves | Average size of reserve |
|---|---|---|---|---|---|---|
| 1 | 12 | 162 | 3146803 | 13 | 15 | 19424 |
| 2 | 15 | 175 | 2616764 | 11 | 11 | 14952 |
| 3 | 13 | 135 | 2139679 | 9 | 7 | 15849 |
| 4 | 11 | 97 | 1985069 | 8 | 2 | 20464 |
| 5 | 9 | 80 | 1727273 | 7 | 3 | 21590 |
| 6 | 6 | 61 | 1879459 | 8 | 3 | 30810 |
| 7 | 4 | 38 | 1336627 | 5 | 2 | 35174 |
| 8 | 4 | 37 | 989859 | 4 | 0 | 26752 |
| 9 | 4 | 25 | 521650 | 2 | 1 | 20866 |
| 10 | 3 | 30 | 1242116 | 5 | 2 | 41403 |
| 11/15 | 8 | 56 | 2765827 | 11 | 0 | 49389 |
| 16/20 | 3 | 22 | 1893439 | 8 | 1 | 86065 |
| Over 20 | 8 | 21 | 2229853 | 9 | 0 | 106183 |
| | 100 | 939 | 24474418 | 100 | 47 | |

SOURCE *Consultative Document on the Future Basis of Premium Assessment,* Table 3 (London, Law Society, November 1982)

only a rather weak relation between the size of claim and the size of practice. However, Table 3.4, which updates this information by including claims resolved between 1979 and 1982, indicates a rather stronger relationship and in particular shows that the average payment on a claim against a firm with more than twenty partners was over £86,000. It should be stressed however that, even three years after the end of the period from which the claims arise, this is a far from complete picture of the final cost to the insurers, as the reserves detailed in Table 3.5 suggest.

Table 3.6 sets out data from which can be calculated (as in column 9) the average payment per partner per £ of 1975 gross fees. The very clear implication of these findings is that sole practitioners are much more vulnerable to claims than partnerships, generating as they do payments of around 5p by way of compensation for each £ of gross fees earned as compared with around 2.5p in the £ for partnerships. The other striking feature is how stable the claims rate remains across partnerships of different sizes once sole practitioners are excluded.

The implication is that larger firms are no more or less careful than small firms once allowance is made for variation in fees. Column 5 of Table 3.6 indicates that partners of large firms are much less likely to be claimed against. This could be a reflection of a number of things: it could be consistent with the exercise of a higher degree of care, better back-up facilities, a superior approach to risk management, or with large firms being able to attract the best solicitors. However, when the larger firms are claimed against, the sum of

Table 3.6  INDEMNITY INSURANCE CLAIMS PAID BY SIZE OF PRACTICE

| c.1<br>Size of firm (number of partners) | c.2<br>number of firms (1976) | c.3<br>number of principals (1976) | c.4<br>number of payments made (1976–79) | c.5<br>=c.4/c.3<br>no. of payments per principal (1976–9) | c.6<br>total payments made (1976/9) £'000 | c.7<br>=c.6/c.3<br>average payment per principal (1976/9) £ | c.8<br>gross fees per partner (1976) £ | c.9<br>=c.7/c.8<br>average payment per principal per £ of 1975 gross fees (1976/9) |
|---|---|---|---|---|---|---|---|---|
| 1 | 2072 | 2072 | 436 | 0.21 | 2,983 | 1,439 | 28,276 | 0.051 |
| 2 | 1699 | 3398 | 372 | 0.11 | 2,471 | 727 | 27,938 | 0.026 |
| 3–4 | 1535 | 5208 | 621 | 0.12 | 3,960 | 760 | 30,551 | 0.025 |
| 5–9 | 897 | 5610 | 409 | 0.07 | 4,501 | 802 | 34,406 | 0.023 |
| 10 or more | 218 | 3087 | 185 | 0.06 | 4,491 | 1,455 | 61,414 | 0.024 |
| Total | 6421 | 19375 | 2032 | 0.10 | 18,406 | 950 | 35,883 | 0.026 |

SOURCE  All data originally from LIB published sources:
(i)   c.2 and c.3 Table 16.5 of *Benson Report* IIb, p 458
(ii)  c.8 from *Benson Report* IIb Table 15.91, p 541
(iii) c.4 and c.6 Table 2 of Law Society *Consultative Document on the Future Basis of Premium Assessment*, November 1982

damages involved is, on average, correspondingly higher, being some three and a half times higher for partnerships of more than ten as compared with sole practitioners.

Our analysis of claims arising from the period 1976–9 made under the Law Society's compulsory Indemnity Scheme suggests that the information available from it is more comprehensive than that generated by other professions, but suffers from disadvantages in that a good number of claims had not been settled by the time of its publication in 1982 and that it is now somewhat out of date. But it does have the great advantage of enabling the researcher to investigate the relationship between size of practice, gross fees and the size of indemnity payments made. The finding that fewer mistakes are made by larger practices, but that indemnity payments are more or less proportional to gross fees falls into the category of what would often be termed 'commercially sensitive' information. It was made available to its members by the Law Society in the course of a consultation exercise on the scheme. Such information is not otherwise routinely published, nor is it available on request. This makes it difficult for the user of legal services to form a reliable judgement as to either how accident-prone solicitors are as a whole or how reliable it is reasonable to expect a large firm to be relative to a small one.

### 3.4.2 Recent Developments in the Solicitors' Indemnity Scheme

As of September 1986 the Law Society's Master Policy for all firms was modified to provide flat cover of £500,000 for each and every claim, although firms continued to take out 'top-up' cover on the private market. The calculation of a firm's basic premium was done by reference to a schedule relating premiums to the gross fees per partner being earned by the practice, rather than as a flat rate as had been the case in the early days of the scheme.

In September 1987 a major change was made to the way in which the scheme is funded. It became a mutual fund run by the profession itself and thus no longer relied on the commercial insurance market. The fund is administered by a company set up expressly for the purpose called Solicitors' Indemnity Fund Ltd., although much of the day-to-day running of the Fund is handled by London Insurance Brokers who had been brokers to the Master Policy scheme.

For the practising solicitor the differences were relatively slight, although premiums have risen quite sharply since the inception of the new arrangements in 1987. The schedule in Table 3.7 sets out the relationship between premiums and earnings per partner for 1988–9. To give an indication of the rise in premiums over the past three years, a practice with gross fees of £50,000 per partner would have paid a basic premium of £1,200 in 1986, £1,620 in 1987 and £1,780 in 1988. It is not possible to establish whether this reflects claims experience in recent years (in terms of either the frequency or size of claims) or whether it reflects something else.

Our analysis of the 1976–9 claims suggests that a premium based on a fixed percentage of gross fees with a loading for sole practitioners would be the fairest approach. The effect of the schedule in Table 3.7 is of course that as fee income per partner rises, the practice pays (overall) a smaller percentage of its

*Table 3.7*  SOLICITORS' INDEMNITY PREMIUMS, 1988

| Gross fees per partner band | | % of gross fees |
| --- | --- | --- |
| Over £ | Up to £ | |
| | 20,000 | 3.6 |
| 20,000 | 30,000 | 3.6 |
| 30,000 | 40,000 | 3.6 |
| 40,000 | 50,000 | 3.4 |
| 50,000 | 60,000 | 3.4 |
| 60,000 | 70,000 | 3.1 |
| 70,000 | 80,000 | 2.8 |
| 80,000 | 90,000 | 2.6 |
| 90,000 | 100,000 | 2.4 |
| 100,000 | 110,000 | 2.2 |
| 110,000 | 120,000 | 2.0 |
| 120,000 | 130,000 | 1.8 |
| 130,000 | 140,000 | 1.6 |
| 140,000 | 150,000 | 1.4 |
| 150,000 | 160,000 | 1.2 |
| 160,000 | 170,000 | 1.0 |
| 170,000 | 180,000 | 0.8 |
| 180,000 | 190,000 | 0.6 |
| 190,000 | 200,000 | 0.4 |
| 200,000 | 220,000 | 0.2 |
| 220,000 | | 0.1 |

SOURCE  Appendix I, *Solicitors' Indemnity Rules, 1988*

fees as premiums. To the extent that fee income per partner tends to increase with the number of partners, this would imply either that large practices have improved, relative to smaller firms, in their claims record, or (less likely) that they are in effect enjoying premium subsidies at the expense of smaller practices.

However these basic premiums are subject to a number of adjustments. One adjustment reflects the principal-staff ratio, for there is a 10 per cent discount on the premium where the number of staff is less than two per principal and a 10 per cent supplement where there are more than five staff per principal. The likely explanation for this is that the degree and quality of supervision of the work of juniors will be higher where there are fewer staff for whom each principal is responsible.

Perhaps more interesting and unusual is the 10 per cent discount available in respect of any practice which has no office situated in a town with a population of 10,000 or more. This small town discount is presumably computed from actuarial data and reflects lower risk exposure. The explanation may be that clients living in small towns are less inclined to sue their solicitors or that small town solicitors are more careful, perhaps because they are less busy.

It is probably not explained by the kind of work such practices do because there is an additional adjustment designed to reflect the fraction of low risk work the practice handles. Criminal law work and work relating to debts of less than £5,000 is classed as low risk, and the more of such work the practice undertakes, the higher the discount. The maximum discount (of 30 per cent of the premium) is available where low risk work accounts for more than 75 per cent of gross fee income.

The loading of premiums in the light of claims experience has also been intensified as compared with the loadings operated in the early days as outlined at the beginning of section 3.4 above. The claims pool (i.e. total value of claims by a practice) is now calculated by reference to 100 per cent of claims in the most recent year, 75 per cent in the previous year and 50 per cent in the first of the three years on which the pool is based. But the loadings now extend to a maximum of 200 per cent of the basic premium for firms whose claims pool exceeds its contributions pool by a factor of 11 or more. A firm with gross fees of £50,000 per partner and such poor claims experience would thus pay a premium of £5,340 as compared with the £1,780 payable by its counterpart experiencing few significant claims. This strongly suggests that a few firms have proved a heavy drain on the insurance fund. Whether it provides an effective deterrent to carelessness is an open question, but it clearly has a significant effect on income levels of the particularly careless.

## 3.5  Concluding Remarks

It is now more than a decade since the Law Society introduced its compulsory indemnity scheme for solicitors. In that time the scheme has evolved considerably from a flat rate premium (with London loading) into a relatively complex premium structure with deductibles, experience rating and other features enabling a discriminating approach to the setting of premiums. The fund now has turnover of around £90 million per annum and accounts for somewhere around four per cent of the gross fee income earned by the profession.

The data generated in the early days of the scheme's operation make it possible to say something about the relative riskiness of different size practices. But lack of data about more recent claims makes it difficult to establish any firm findings as to whether the pattern of claims has remained stable, and in particular whether the changing structure of premiums has had the effect one might have predicted on claims.

# 4　Accountants and Architects

## 4.1　Introduction

In this chapter we consider two professions with similar characteristics—
accountants and architects. In both, services are provided through a market by
professional firms which in the great majority of instances are organised as
partnerships. Accordingly, many of the practitioners in these firms will have
incomes which contain a profit-sharing element, so that they have an incentive
to control costs and revenues. We shall be concerned to show that liability rules
are more likely to be an important influence in such an environment than they
will in circumstances where those who provide services are simply salaried
employees. This argument can of course also be applied to the legal profession
examined in the previous chapter.

## 4.2　Accountants

In England and Wales, there are two main groupings of accountants. Certified
Accountants are relatively less numerous than Chartered Accountants, and
tend to be smaller firms (many being Sole Practitioners). At present there are
some 14,500 firms of Chartered Accountants compared with less than 3,000
firms of Certified Accountants. The latter tend to deal with a narrower range
of work (particularly auditing and personal tax work) whilst Chartered
Accountants deal with a broader range of work, extending very often into
management consultancy. Turnover and profits of Chartered Accountants are
generally rather higher, and their exposure to professional liability claims
correspondingly higher.

### 4.2.1　Certified Accountants

Since 1980 it has been compulsory for firms belonging to the Association of
Certified Accountants (ACA) to have approved indemnity insurance. The
Association has its own scheme run by a firm of brokers to which members may
belong. It will recognise policies offered by certain other insurers as well, and
indeed supplies to accountants seeking a practising certificate a list of (five or
so) other brokers specialising in professional indemnity insurance. When firms
make their annual application for renewal of their practising certificate they

are required to supply the name of their insurer and the policy number. Without evidence of cover they cannot obtain the right to practice.

The amount of indemnity cover required is not specified by the Association. Most brokers are unwilling to quote for cover of less than £50,000. In their information to applicants for practising certificates the Association offer the following advice about an adequate level of cover:

> ... [the level] must reflect the type and nature of work undertaken by the particular practice and should include an honest appraisal by the principal or partners of the financial harm which could be suffered by the largest client and the legal expenses which could be incurred were any error to occur in the conduct of the practice. As a very general rule, experience indicates that the limit of indemnity should be not less than two and one half times the annual fee income of the practice.

Under the Association's scheme the basic premium for cover of £100,000 was around £300 in 1988. Cover for higher levels of indemnity is obviously more expensive, although the premium does not increase in proportion to the height of the ceiling. Interestingly, the spread of premiums charged to different firms increases sharply with the amount of coverage. Safer firms are, in effect, offered much greater discounts on higher levels of cover than on low ones. The principal determinant of the premium charged to a company is the structure of its workload. Companies relying heavily on taxation work, management consultancy, insolvency work or investment work can expect higher premiums. Companies heavily reliant on a single client or having a high number of staff per partner can also expect to pay more.

It is apparently rare for a firm to experience difficulty in finding indemnity insurance, although it is true that if a firm were unable to get cover it would not be able to obtain a practising certificate. An individual broker will sometimes decline to insure particular sorts of risk, preferring to specialise perhaps in larger practices.

### 4.2.2  Chartered Accountants

Until very recently firms of Chartered Accountants were free to make whatever arrangements they wished as to indemnity insurance. The insurance market for accountants works in the same way as it does for other professional groups such as architects and solicitors. Premiums reflect the volume of work done by a practice, its past claims record and so on. The Appendix to this work contains a reproduction (by kind permission of Nelson Hurst & Marsh Ltd, a leading Lloyd's Broker in the field of professional indemnity insurance) of the Proposal Form to be filled in by firms of accountants seeking indemnity insurance. It will be immediately obvious from the form that the broker asks for a relatively detailed breakdown of the firm's past record and its current activities before being prepared to offer insurance.

However, increasing litigation and a desire to reassure prospective clients has caused the Institute of Chartered Accountants (ICA) to introduce, as from the beginning of 1989 and for some firms 1990, a new compulsory scheme for its members. Under this new scheme, referred to as the 'Professional Indemnity Insurance Regulations' firms seeking to obtain or renew practising certificates must be able to demonstrate that they carry a minimum level of indemnity insurance cover with an approved insurer. The minimum amount of cover deemed compulsory will be calculated as the higher of £50,000 for a sole practitioner (or £100,000 for a partnership) and two and a half times gross fee income. The maximum cover required under these rules will be £500,000, although firms will remain free to exceed this cover limit if they wish. Indeed it is recommended that practices should take out additional cover above half a million pounds cover amounting to 2.5 times annual gross fee income or 25 times the largest single fee, whichever is the larger.

A list of around forty underwriters approved by the ICA will offer indemnity insurance along these lines, although they will be perfectly able to discriminate amongst firms in terms of the conditions of insurance and the premiums they charge. These same underwriters will also contribute, in proportion to their premium income, to an Assigned Risks Pool. This Pool, at least initially, will offer insurance to firms unable to obtain it through any of the underwriters in the usual way. It will thus carry the poorest risks, although, not surprisingly, premiums for firms insuring through the Pool will be on the high side.

Firms unable to find insurance through the approved underwriters and forced into the Pool will be investigated by the Institute's Practice Regulation Directorate at the firm's expense. If this investigation indicates that the public or the firm's clients are in jeopardy, action may be taken to prevent or limit the firm's activities. After a maximum of twenty four months in the Pool the firm, if it still cannot obtain cover outside the Pool, will be excluded from cover by the Pool. Thus any failure to improve sufficiently will mean that the firm loses its right to practice as Chartered Accountants

Although the careless firm may survive for a while, a bad practice record will in the final analysis exclude it from practice. This is a very powerful sanction for the Institute to have and to exercise, From the profession's point of view however it may be an effective way of inducing firms to act with a high degree of care, and this will prove a good investment if it enables this section of the accountancy profession to enhance its reputation for delivering a high quality service to its clients. It will also ensure that the demands placed on the Pool do not become excessive.

This Pool arrangement will have the same kind of cross-subsidising effect as other schemes such as those of the medical defence societies. The underwriter knows that the more business he writes for firms of accountants the higher will be his liability to contribute to the Pool. This contribution will increase the underwriter's costs and will therefore be reflected in the terms on which he is prepared to offer indemnity to the firm outside the Assigned Risks Pool (ARP). The 'safer' firm can thus expect to be paying higher premiums than it would in the absence of the ARP. In practice, of course, it would be hoped that only a minimal number of firms will be forced into the Pool and thus its demands for financial support kept to a minimum.

It is inevitable that such burden as the regulations represent will ultimately be paid for in large part by the clients of firms of Chartered Accountants, since the costs of insurance will be shifted on to them in the form of higher fees. However, the degree to which such costs can be passed on will depend to some degree on the view taken by clients as to how much risk they are prepared to take. A reputation for higher quality service, and better protection in the event of the firm making errors, than that which is available from other kinds of accountancy firms is only valuable if clients are prepared to pay for it.

Competition between rival groupings within a profession will tend to drive indemnity insurance arrangements into line with clients' perceptions of how elaborate and costly they ought to be. It is thus interesting to observe that the ICA is now following the lead of the ACA in making cover compulsory. Whether this is a defensive move to prevent a loss of clients by firms of Chartered Accountants is difficult to guage, but at least it seems reasonable to conclude at least that clients appear to want more rather than less indemnity insurance cover.

## 4.2.3 The Organisation of Accountancy Firms

An important influence on how the firm providing professional services responds to the professional liability regime is its internal organisation. Since even the large professional firms are organised as partnerships, it is important to explore the implications of this otherwise relatively uncommon structure. The standard analysis, following developments in the theory of property rights, suggests that the claimants to residual earnings (i.e. the firm's profits) will be those most concerned to ensure that decisions are in line with the objective of profit maximisation. Salaried employees or managers, by contrast, when exercising discretion in decision making may be inclined to favour steps which promote their own interests at the expense of shareholder profits.

Professional partnerships avoid this potential conflict of interest by fusing the functions of ownership and control. The practitioner supplies to the firm both labour services and risk capital, with the result that his income will contain both a salary element and a share of the practice's profits or losses. It follows from this that any individual partner can be thought of as having an interest in both ensuring that his own actions are consistent with maximisation of the firm's profits *and* that the actions of the other partners are so directed.

The advantage this bestows in terms of the firm's profitability may be offset by some drawbacks. Any investment or expansion of the firm has to be financed by its partners, and this can prove a heavy burden particularly if the benefits are not expected immediately. The more senior partners may be reluctant to plough ever larger sums into the practice if they are nearing retirement age, since it may be difficult to arrange for them to be assured of benefiting from the goodwill (the capitalised future profits) the investment creates.

The other inhibition to expansion of partnerships lies in the dilution of the partner's share in profits as new partners are taken on. His own income becomes less sensitive to the profit consequences of his own decisions, and he is likely to find it increasingly difficult to monitor effectively the behaviour of his copartners. There are, of course, ways of overcoming this 'loss of control' problem. The most popular, and one which is widely used in the larger firms of accountants (and also solicitors) is the creation of cost centres.

Different activities, e.g. auditing, tax planning and so on, are identified within the practice and each activity or centre becomes responsible for its own profit position. The fee income it earns is used to pay for the centre's own direct costs and for the transfer of any services provided centrally within the firm. A residual or profit element can thus be identified for each cost centre. The incomes of partners will be adjusted to reflect the profitability of the cost centres with which they are associated as well as that of the business as a whole.

This kind of arrangement has a number of advantages, particularly in the context of large, rapidly-growing firms offering an ever wider range of services. As well as giving the partner a renewed sense of the link between his own actions and income, it will concentrate attention on the allocation of resources within the firm. Space, equipment, secretarial resources, etc, can all be priced and traded in an internal market in such a way as to encourage their use in the most profitable possible way.

The continuing struggle by those with an interest in the firm's profitability to keep decisions along profit-maximising lines will be valued by the proponent of a negligence rule. Achievement of an efficient degree of care in the provision of professional services is more likely if the signals created by the liability rule impinge on profit-oriented practitioners rather than on salaried employees who may be relatively indifferent to profitability. Profit-sharing practitioners will engage in defensive work up to, but not beyond, the point at which it is cost-justified, whereas the salary earner may be 'too careful' or 'insufficiently careful' depending on how thoroughly his behaviour is monitored and the degree (if any) to which his income is performance related.

Of course, the achievement of an efficient degree of care requires not only that the practitioner's income be sensitive to the degree of care he exercises, but also that the 'correct' signals are being sent by the judges hearing negligence cases. This will happen provided that they apply the correct standard of care in determining questions of liability and award appropriate sums of damages. As we will now show, however, the role of the firm's reputation in the market may be at least as important an influence on its choice of degree of care as a liability rule.

### 4.2.4  Risk Management and the Accountancy Firm

Accountancy firms, particularly the very large firms of Chartered Accountants with extensive networks of branches and associations with firms of accountants overseas, are very conscious of their vulnerability to loss of reputation. Any suggestion of carelessness can have a dramatic effect on the firm's capacity to attract and retain clients, as one of the major firms found to its cost in the wake of the Johnson Mathey scandal.[1] The major firms as a result accord priority to efforts to ensure the quality and reliability of their work.

These efforts find expression in various forms. Preparation of manuals detailing procedures, internal audits to ensure that these procedures are followed and (internal) investigations of instances where liability claims are made or where 'near misses' are recorded are all fairly standard. These explicit devices used to monitor and control the firm's risk exposure are in place because they make a positive contribution to profitability. But it is important to be clear that there are at least three channels through which the degree of care exercised can impinge on profits. The first is through the costs of care, as emphasised in Chapter 1. The other two we have thus far treated together simply as the cost of damage. We distinguish here that part of the damage which is in the form of compensation for clients (or equivalently for indemnity insurance premiums) and that part which is in the form of loss of reputation and the resulting contraction in demand for the firm's services.

It may not have escaped the reader's notice, however, that if prospective clients are well informed about the quality of work (or the degree of care) to be expected from different firms then the liability rule may actually be largely redundant. If careless firms lose clients, then there is only a limited role for liability to damages since such firms will have poor survival qualities. But of course clients may often find it difficult or costly to establish the relative reliability of different practitioners. In such a world, the *signalling function* of the negligence rule may be of particular value, since the very bringing of an action by a dissatisfied client conveys information which can be gathered relatively cheaply by others who are searching for a reputable firm.

The force of this argument may be weakened a little by the likelihood that the firm thus threatened may have a very great incentive to find ways of settling any claim before it comes to court so as to avoid the attendant publicity. Any loss in signal power is mitigated by the fact that the firm's insurers, and not the firm itself, will be responsible for meeting the cost of settlements, and they may not be as concerned with the potential loss of reputation to the firm as with the costs to themselves of settlement. However, insurers themselves can get a bad reputation if they pursue their own interest at the expense of that of the insured. The insurer will not necessarily therefore always pursue a strategy of minimising costs when handling a claim if by doing so he risks alienating the insured and possibly other potential customers.

At the end of the day the firm of accountants may be anxious to guard against actions for professional liability more because of the threat they represent to revenues than because of the extra costs the firm will face in terms of a loading of its premiums for indemnity.

## 4.3  Architects

Architects may be liable for damages as result of breach of contract or because of the commission of a tort. Clearly an architect has a professional commitment to fulfil his contract. Beyond this, however, he has a wider responsibility: he cannot ignore the common law duty of care for the well-being of others who might suffer as a consequence of his actions. Cecil (1984, p7) notes that this wider responsibility is covered in the Royal Institute of British Architects' Code of Conduct where reference is made to an architect's responsibility to 'those who will use and enjoy his buildings'. This wider liability is covered by the common law of tort, so that for example, if a passer-by were to be injured by falling masonry from a building, the architect in question could be the subject of a law suit. If the owner of the building had fulfilled his duties of maintenance then the architect may be liable either because of failure to supervise the builder or because of design error.

The market in indemnity insurance for architects has seen many of the changes already noted in this study. Since 1945 most members of the RIBA have carried professional indemnity insurance, though while cover varied, few firms carried as much as £250,000 and some indemnities were as low as £10,000. In the 1960s the effect of a building boom and the less personal relationship between architect and client appeared to increase the likelihood of a claim. By the 1970s claims were a matter of increasing concern, the average cost of indemnity insurance at this time being between $\frac{1}{2}$ per cent and 1 per cent of gross fees earned in the preceding year.[2] However, in the mid-1970s the courts, through a series of key judgements, which pointed to an extension of professional liability, made the task of indemnity insurers far more difficult. With awards and settlements reaching unprecedented levels, some insurers, including a US company which had been insuring a majority of architects, withdrew from the market.[3] They were replaced by other brokers but in the wake of these changes there was a substantial rise in premiums for many firms. By 1983, on average, architects were paying 3 per cent of gross fees earned in the preceding year. Currently the average figure would be about 7 per cent, though for small firms it can be as much as 9–12 per cent. What is evident in these figures is that: (a) the cost of indemnity insurance has risen steeply as a proportion of gross fees; and (b) the variation in the fees is marked and increasing.

The rise in the costs of indemnity insurance surely reflects, at least in part, the growth in the number of claims. In 1979 there was one claim for every seven indemnity insurance policies. In 1987 there were seven claims for every 10 indemnity insurance policies. It is still the case that, to some extent, there is cross-subsidisation among policies. Even so, there certainly appears to be an increasing effort to relate the indemnity insurance policy and premium to the characteristics of the professional practitioner in this market.

The level of indemnity required is not uniform among practices. The Royal Institute of British Architects has not yet made insurance a compulsory condition of membership but recommends most strongly that all practitioners, including part-time ones, should be properly insured. It is unlikely that any practice will have less than £100,000 cover and the annual cost of professional indemnity insurance to this amount is about £1,000. It is said that many clients of architects will not accept services by firms which have less than £250,000 worth of cover and, indeed, that in the case of some clients (such as High Street firms) this requirement could be as much as £5 million. The awareness of clients as to the coverage of firms in this market is a notable feature and in marked contrast to that in other professional markets.

Typically firms of architects are advised to insure between two and three times the annual gross fee income (including VAT) declared by the practice in the previous financial year. In 1984 they were advised to keep a minimum limit of £250,000: see Cecil (1984). There is no standard professional indemnity policy and architects are assessed on the basis of a quite detailed proposal form. One of the considerations is the type of client that the practice is likely to take on. Housing Associations are considered high risk clients and hospitals, structural surveys and special one-off projects of a technical nature will be seen as of higher risk. In these cases, insurance premiums may be increased as much as 50 per cent to 100 per cent on the basic level of premium as a reflection of expected future losses. The RIBA Insurance Agency Statistics for claims made in 1986 showed a pattern of claims by client groups as set out in Table 4.1.

## 4.3.1 Architects and the role of negligence

What evidence is there to suggest that the market has deterred professional negligence and generally educated practitioners? While it is not argued that the market for indemnity insurance is as competitive as would be desirable, there is some reason to believe that competition between insurance and underwriters has had the expected results.

In the first place, there is an attempt to relate insurance premiums to expected future losses. It has already been noted that architects must declare the nature of their business when submitting insurance proposal forms. Perhaps more important as a disciplining factor, they must also declare their claims experience. In a discussion of indemnity insurance proposal forms Cecil (1984) considers questions which appear 'on all the most common forms' (p 112). In section 3.3.18 he notes: 'The form will ask for details on all claims (successful or not) made in the past 10 years against the practice or its present and/or past partners.' He duly advises practitioners that while, if they remain with one company, they might reply that the information is known to that company, they must, when seeking competitive quotations 'remember that answering this question fully and accurately is absolutely crucial' (p 117), since insurance contracts will normally be void if there is evidence of non-disclosure to the insurer of relevant information.

*Table 4.1*   CLAIMS BY CLIENT GROUPS (1986)

| Client groups | Percentage of claims |
| --- | --- |
| Offices | 23.8 |
| Houses | 22.1 |
| Shops | 8.6 |
| Factories | 8.4 |
| Flats | 8.2 |
| Hospitals | 4.8 |

SOURCE   N T Pepperell, *Liability Update: Professional Risk Avoidance* (RIBAIR Indemnity Research Ltd, 1988, p 18)

*Table 4.2*   NOTIFICATION OF CLAIMS RECORDED BY RIBA INSURANCE AGENCY
(1.4.86–31.3.87)

| | Causes by group | % of all | Cum % |
|---|---|---|---|
| 1 | Design errors or faults attributed to the design | 12.1 | 12.1 |
| 2 | Roofs | 11.2 | 23.3 |
| 3 | Walls | 7.0 | 30.3 |
| 4 | Floors | 4.8 | 35.1 |
| 5 | Supervision | 4.6 | 39.7 |
| 6 | Damp | 4.2 | 43.9 |
| 7 | Delay to Contract | 3.9 | 47.8 |
| 8 | Planning | 3.7 | 51.5 |
| 9 | Certification, Extra Costs, Glazing | 10.5 | 62.0 |
| 10 | Foundations | 3.1 | 65.1 |
| 11 | Leaks | 2.7 | 67.8 |
| 12 | Heating failures, Surveys | 4.8 | 72.6 |
| 13 | Cladding | 1.8 | 74.4 |
| 14 | Brickwork | 1.7 | 76.1 |
| 15 | Drainage | 1.5 | 77.6 |
| 16 | Fee recovery, Accidents | 2.6 | 80.2 |
| 17 | Dry rot, Accidents on site | 2.2 | 82.4 |
| 18 | Ceilings, Doors, Gutters, Lifts, Tiles | 4.6 | 87.0 |
| 19 | Car parks, Noise | 1.5 | 88.5 |
| 20 | Copyright, Fans, Showers, Wrong Plants, Cables, DPC | 3.3 | 91.8 |
| 21 | Boundaries, Chimneys, Fire, Insulation, Kitchens, Pipework, Stairs | 2.6 | 94.4 |
| 22 | Other general causes | 5.6 | 100 |

SOURCE *Architects' Liability* (October, 1987, p2)

In the second place, there is reason to believe that indemnity insurance premiums, identified by the Royal Institute of British Architects Indemnity Research, offer practitioners evidence of the liability to which they are exposed. [The Royal Institute of British Architects are funding the research work which is being done by RIBA Indemnity Research. This work is designed to identify the causes of claims in order to use this information for risk avoidance. Policy holders are advised as to how to reduce future liability as a result of this research.]

The result is that the market appears informed about the nature of the problems which arise in architects' practices. The causes of problems are identified in Table 4.2. It is known, for example, that design errors were the top of the list with respect to claims made to the RIBA Insurance Agency during the period 1 April 1986 to 31 March 1987.

## 4.3.2  Future Directions in Architects' Liability

Another consequence of the market pressures created by negligence is the emergence of a proposal for a scheme of peer review. Currently architects are considering introducing a scheme designed to reduce the vulnerability of practices to claims. The scheme has already been promoted by the American Institute of Architects in the United States.

A visit is made by a panel of reviewers to an architect's practice. The visit usually by three reviewers may last one or two or three days depending on the size of the practice to be reviewed. The cost to a small firm in the USA is about $2,000, though, as most of this is to cover travelling expenses, it is envisaged that the costs would be lower in the UK. The reviewers focus on administrative procedures, where typically there is considerable room for tightening up in ways which will reduce exposure to claims for negligence. Cecil (1988) suggests that similar weaknesses (e.g. with respect to fee agreements and details of commissions) must exist in the UK. It is envisaged that insurers could offer premium discounts for firms regularly inviting peer review.

While architects are also concerned with the adversarial nature of the situation being created between client and professional when claims for negligence are made, to be realistic, they are not able to propose a move to a strict liability basis. There is little prospect of arranging indemnity insurance via a state-financed scheme and proposals which have been made are therefore in terms of a return to what we have termed 'caveat emptor' in earlier chapters.

Quite recently a report of the Insurance Feasibility Steering Committee (IFSC) has produced a strong recommendation for Building User Insurance against Latent Defects (BUILD). This scheme would involve the building owner taking out insurance prior to construction with any risk being on cover for ten years and transferable to subsequent owners. As far as the producers of the building—contractors, subcontractors and designers—were concerned, they would be named in the insurance and held safe from subsequent pursuit by the insurers.

The advantages of this scheme are said to be derived from the likelihood that the architect would be more concerned with the task of redressing the problem than with defending his position. Furthermore, the costs of negligence cases might therefore be reduced. The view of the committee was that, at the end of the day, the costs of insurance would fall on the client, irrespective of whether he actually paid for it directly or whether he paid for it in the costs of the architect.

## 4.4 Concluding Remarks

Professional indemnity insurance has become a matter of increasing concern for both architects and accountants. According to a survey conducted in 1988 Chartered Accountants can expect to pay between 3 per cent and 3.6 per cent of gross fee income averaged over the last five years for cover of £250,000 in the aggregate. Architects, who in the 1970s were paying less than 1 per cent of gross fees for indemnity insurance can now expect to pay between 6 per cent and 12 per cent of the previous year's gross fee income for cover of £500,000. Many practices will seek higher levels of cover and will in any event be liable to deductibles of 2 per cent or so of gross fees. The overall cost of liability insurance, including this element of self insurance, is thus considerable and has grown sharply in  relation to fees.

As one would expect when so many of these practices are organised as sole traders or partnerships, an active approach is taken by many practices towards risk management in an effort to keep down the cost of indemnity premiums. It will not normally be possible to infer whether these efforts are motivated by keeping down premiums or by the desire to maintain an unblemished reputation for high quality service. For most purposes, this does not matter: the clients' desires for quality will prevail one way or the other.

The market for indemnity insurance is certainly very sensitive to a practice's claims record, suggesting that some practices have a consistently poor record. Architects are seeking to address this problem by peer review to identify weakness in procedures. Amongst firms of accountants, it has been suggested to us, the larger practices make strenuous efforts through internal control devices to minimise errors whilst smaller firms may be more casual. Certainly the professional accountancy bodies are taking liability seriously, and both now have compulsory schemes. It remains to be seen whether rising standards will emerge in the wake of the increasing propensity of dissatisfied clients to litigate.

## NOTES

1   Following the Johnson Mathey banking company's collapse there was criticism of lack of effective financial control of the company and, at least by implication, criticism of the major accountancy firm involved. For some time, accountants in question suffered badly and found it difficult to attract and retain clients.
2   The authors are grateful for the assistance of Mr Neil Pepperel in assisting with the provision of this information.
3   Cecil (1984, p108) points out that one company, ABS Insurance Agency Ltd, provided insurance for 65 per cent of practices and APIA (Architects & Professional Indemnity Agency) provided another 15 per cent. Other policies were available through companies at Lloyds, many of them dealing with bad claims records.

# 5 Conclusions and Policy Recommendations

## 5.1 Introduction

In recent years there has clearly been an increase in litigation over professional liability matters in the UK, both in terms of claims frequency and damages awarded. It is not unnatural, therefore, that the professions have responded by suggesting amendments and reform of current practices. Indeed, in 1986 the Department of Trade and Industry (DTI) undertook a review of whether there should be any limitation to damages and to negligence litigation generally. While recognising the increasing strains upon indemnity insurance which had been created by an increasingly litigatious climate, the DTI refrained from any major limitation on current practices. It suggested that professions should engage in tighter quality control, that they might utilise mutual insurance arrangements and, finally, that professionals might negotiate with insurers for reduced premiums for 'clean claims' records (Hay, 1987).

This study shows that increased litigation has prompted different professional groups to consider alternative indemnity insurance arrangements. The desire to remove the adversarial nature of the professional-client relationship which emerges in cases of negligence has become a spur to proposed reforms, or at least has become part of the rhetoric in which such proposals are made. The British Medical Association has advocated a no-fault scheme, in part for this reason, whilst in similar vein architects are suggesting a move towards 'caveat emptor', leaving clients to take up the issue of compensation directly with their own insurers.

That professionals would wish to effect changes which insulate them from the effects of increased litigation is hardly surprising. The call from the professions for limitations by the DTI can be rationalised on the lines that consumers have come to expect 'too much' from professionals (Hay, 1987). However, for policy purposes the important point which emerges from this study is that there is a distinction between the issue of whether damages and claims are 'too great' and whether professionals should remain within the law of negligence. Whether clients expect 'too much' is only part of the story.

As a means of assessing current and proposed practices for dealing with professional liability, this study has utilised the framework established by Calabresi (1970), by identifying three aspects of any system for dealing with accidents, namely: (a) efficiency and deterrence; (b) compensation and loss spreading; and (c) administrative and transactions costs. Earlier chapters have demonstrated that such considerations are by no means independent of one another: many policy changes will impinge on more than one aspect, and very often will look attractive using one criterion but not others.

A balanced appraisal will require that all criteria should be employed. Public policy recommendations which focus on a single criterion (e.g. minimising administrative and transactions costs) may be called into question when their full effects are analysed. For example, it may be that a new procedure could reduce the administrative and transactions costs *per case* when dealing with negligence but weaken the deterrent effect. The total number of cases may therefore rise so that *total* administrative and transactions costs actually increase. This is an important conclusion and one to which we shall return.

In the course of the study we have identified three main classes of liability rule which feature in the contemporary debate about professional liability. These were:

(i) a negligence rule under which a person suffering harm as a result of behaviour by a professional practitioner can recover damages, provided that he can demonstrate that the loss was a consequence of the practitioner's failure to exercise a reasonable degree of care;

(ii) a strict liability (or 'no-fault') rule under which a person suffering harm may recover damages irrespective of how careful or careless the practitioner was;

(iii) a no liability (or 'caveat emptor') rule under which the person suffering harm is liable for his own losses, which he may opt to cover through a first party insurance contract.

It is important to recall also that these are not the only devices through which some degree of control can be exercised over the quality of service available from professional practitioners. Many professions have their own committees for ensuring that professional standards are maintained; there may be external regulation of standards by government-appointed agencies and there may also be machinery within the criminal law which can be used in certain circumstances. We have concentrated on the use of liability rules in this study, but in practice these will be only a part of a mix of controls.

The main arguments and findings can now be drawn together using Calabresi's framework. We ask the question: what can be said about each criterion and what directions are indicated for public policy? Compared with much of the popular writing in this area our answers concentrate heavily on the efficiency and administrative aspects at the expense of discussion of loss-spreading. As far as the latter is concerned, we would argue that even here efficiency (in terms of the operation of insurance markets) is important and often given less weight than it merits.

## 5.2   Education, Deterrence and Efficiency

As far as this first criterion is concerned the central issue is whether professionals learn from the information produced by court decisions and whether such a learning process is desirable.

It is clearly important that the professional is *not* insulated from court decisions which may be relevant to practice. Information about the consequences of exercising different degrees of care is essential if the decision taker is to be confronted with correct incentives. If there is no mechanism through which professionals may be called to account it is not clear how their behaviour can be influenced for the better. To this extent we believe that there is good reason to endorse the recommendations of the DTI, i.e. that, where possible, greater use should be made of claims-related indemnity insurance premiums. In this study it is evident that, where the disincentive to be careless increases, the professional appears to alter behaviour to avoid negligence.

The use of information such as claims experience has been a major concern in this study. While recognising the non-pecuniary costs that practitioners inevitably incur as a result of being the subject of malpractice suits, the logic of the current insurance arrangements dictates that if problems of moral hazard are to be overcome then information about future losses of practitioners must be incorporated in insurance premiums, for this is the mechanism through which the practice will feel the effects of court decisions.

We have already shown that where there are signals which enable good practice to be rewarded, professionals take steps to improve the quality of their product. Where professionals' reputations are at stake, for example, professional practices exercise more care to avoid errors. Where, as in the case of law and accountancy firms, reputation is important, practices and procedures are amended so as to reduce the probability of actions for negligence. In Chapter 3 it was shown that larger law firms, where reputation is likely to be significant, experience lower claims rates. Moves to make greater use of peer and management review in the NHS through medical audit should make doctors more sensitive to errors or bad practice, with similarly beneficial results.

However, where clients have neither the incentive nor the opportunity to collect information about the quality of service the sanction of increased indemnity insurance may act as an alternative to loss of business through poor reputation as a way of penalising the careless practitioner. As a corollary, we infer that liability rules are particularly important in markets where consumers might otherwise find difficulty in monitoring and/or controlling the quality of service they get. The informational asymmetry in markets for professional services is a consequence of the difficulties and costs to clients of assembling information about service quality. A liability rule does not solve or eliminate this asymmetry but it does at least limit the professional's capacity to exploit it to his own advantage.

This temptation for an individual practitioner to mislead clients, and ultimately to mar the reputation of his profession is of course the principal motivation for professions to engage in effective self-regulation. We have ignored this aspect of the professions in our study, but it is as well to reiterate the interdependence of devices to control the quality of professional services.

The mode of organisation within professional firms also can be interpreted as a means of encouraging the practitioner to take service quality seriously. Following the standard property rights approach to the theory of the firm (see for example Jensen and Meckling, 1976 or the work of Williamson, 1964, on managerial discretion) it has been argued that partners, who are paid a share of the firm's profits, will have a greater incentive to minimise costs (e.g. by monitoring the quality of their own work and that of their colleagues in the firm more closely) than employees or managers who are paid a fixed salary. In so far as indemnity insurance premiums add to costs and thus reduce the net revenue of the firm, it is clear that decision makers in the firm may have a greater incentive to avoid negligence if they are organised as a partnership. Firms of solicitors (and practices in a number of other professions) are generally so organised, and this may be in part because of the superior capacity of such organisations to control quality.

We have illustrated this argument for several professions, including the case of architects, where the indemnity insurance premium is determined with reference to the nature of the practice and claims experience. Each firm of architects then has a stimulus to assess performance and to set its fee structure so as to reflect the risks posed by different client groups. The Royal Institute of British Architects have sponsored a research body to locate the causes of negligence claims and to advise architects accordingly in order to assist them to take steps which reduce the cost of indemnity insurance. Schemes have been established for architects whereby they voluntarily seek peer review in order to see whether or not their practice can be modified in order to improve the standard of service and thereby reduce indemnity insurance premiums.

In the case of chartered accountants, premiums again depend upon the work undertaken and the claims record of the practice. Persistent negligence will make it impossible for a firm to find indemnity insurance cover, forcing it into a Pool and leaving it open to investigation by the Institute's Practice Regulation Directorate. If, after twenty four months, the firm still cannot secure insurance it will be excluded from the pool and thereby lose its right to practise. The stimulus to re-consider the standard of service offered is obvious in the extreme situation, whereby failure to approach the expected norms of professional practice may lead to closure.

In the case of medical practitioners, insurance premiums are not claims-related. There still remain the non-pecuniary costs of making serious errors (discussed in Chapter 2) and these are likely to be a significant deterrent to negligence. Therefore we have argued that, if there were to be a move away from negligence and towards no-fault or strict liability, there would need to be clear proposals as to how medical practitioners would be 'called to account' if they make avoidable errors.

The overall impression to be drawn from these individual studies is that claims-related indemnity insurance, or some alternative form of sanction should apply. Indeed, it would be a matter for disquiet if schemes were introduced which attenuated both the flow of information and the disincentive for professionals to act with 'reasonable' care. However, this is not to say that professionals are (or ought to be) liable for all accidents or for the unrealised expectations of their clients. Under the law of contract and the law of negligence they are only liable for those actions which can be proven to result from the lack of reasonable care.

A great many consumers insulate themselves from a variety of risks through insurance (e.g. against fire, loss of life, losses when on holiday etc) and it is perfectly possible to argue that they should be expected to acquire additional (first party) insurance cover against the adverse outcomes which may result even when professionals act with reasonable care. To this extent the professional is quite entitled to expect that clients acquire their own insurance. On the other hand there is no reason to suppose that, when courts act responsibly, the current incentive mechanisms, as they relate to negligence, should not operate. Although the climate now favours litigation, this in itself does not lend any weight to the case for policy reform which marginalises signals and disincentives. If awards are 'too high' and the number of cases 'too many', the focus of attention should be on the information which is created, not on removing or dampening incentive mechanisms.

While the DTI chose, in 1986, not to add limitations to the litigation process, Parliament in the same year introduced the Latent Damages Act. This dealt with the period of time over which professionals could be held liable. The Act has two main effects: (1) to limit the period between becoming aware of negligence and bringing a negligence suit to three years; (2) to limit negligence to a fifteen year period so that, whether or not individuals are aware of negligence, they cannot bring actions arising from events more than fifteen years previously. This legislation was controversial, particularly with architects who argued that fifteen years was excessive. Consumers by contrast would argue that there are no grounds for any such limitation. The act represents a compromise between producer and consumer interests but not a significant breach of liability on the part of professionals. The case for such limitation is based on equity and 'fairness' to both parties, which, as a rule, one would expect to find in court decisions. However, the deterrent effect of the tort system is obviously not greatly reduced by this legislation.

The above arguments have been concerned with the transmission of signals. Economic efficiency does of course depend on signals having the 'correct' content as well as being transmitted effectively. There are generally two key questions in any instance where professional negligence is alleged, viz. (1) was the professional acting with a reasonable degree of care? (the *liability* issue) and (2) if not, how much damage has the plaintiff suffered? (the *quantum* issue). From an efficiency perspective it is important that both these issues are decided appropriately by courts. The rules we would want to see followed are:

(1) *negligence should be considered as proven when it is clear that the professional failed to exercise a degree of care on behalf of the client which would be warranted by a realistic assessment of the benefits in relation to the costs of so doing;* and

(2) *the amount of compensation should correspond to the losses that the client has experienced as a result of such failure.*

These recommendations are very much standard in the law and economics literature and in keeping with the so-called Learned Hand formula although they are not universally followed by English courts. We have illustrated how adherence to this principle would minimise the sum of damage costs and resource costs of care.

In Chapter 2 we argued that judgements as to negligence should be left ultimately to the courts. We rejected the notion that professional standards should be set solely by the profession. Courts must, of course, defer to professional opinion but should also be able to apply an external standard based on a cost/benefit calculation.

In England the test for negligence has been related to a ruling in a medical action of some thirty years ago brought by a Mr Bolam. The trial judge referred to the following definition:

> The test is the standard of the ordinary skilled man exercising and professing to have that special skill. A man need not possess the highest skill. It is well-established law that it is sufficient if he exercises the ordinary skill of an ordinary competent man exercising that particular art. . . . (Jackson, 1988, p 537)

While this ruling has guided many professional negligence cases over the past thirty years, there is good reason to believe that its interpretation has been different in different cases. On the one hand, it has been argued that it is not for a trial judge to question professional opinion, so that if the defence could argue that certain practices were acceptable to some professionals, this was a sufficient defence. On the other hand, (particularly solicitors' negligence cases) courts have attached less weight in other cases to the evidence of professionals. Negligence in conveyancing, for example, has been found to have occurred even when the performance of the defendant accorded with current practices (Jackson, 1988).

While we would argue in favour of consistency, our view is that ultimately court decisions (as to liability) should be related to the ruling of Judge Learned Hand, i.e. by reference to the costs and benefits relevant to the professional's action rather than to prevailing professional practice. The purpose of liability from an economic perspective is to encourage professionals to exercise a 'cost-justified' degree of care, not just to encourage all to behave in the same way. Whether, in general, courts have abided by *this* principle and whether or not court decisions have become more generous in applying it, is a question which would require much more extended treatment. Nevertheless, we believe that for policy purposes recommendation (1) will prove an important benchmark.

This leaves us with the question of the quantum of damages. If correct assessment of quantum is an essential component of efficient signals from the courts, it can be regarded as an efficiency concern. More often, however, quantum is thought of as an equity matter. For if victims are 'undercompensated' under negligence, as is often argued (e.g. Harris *et al.,* 1984), then it fails to distribute the losses from accidents equitably.

## 5.3   Compensation

The second criterion by which to judge any system of dealing with accidents centres on the arrangements for distributing losses. In the case of professional liability this requires investigation as to whether the practitioner or the client is responsible, in the first instance, for the losses and the degree to which any broader loss spreading is possible. In a world of well-developed insurance markets there may be a small problem because any agent, whether client or practitioner, will generally be able to buy insurance cover. There are however some circumstances where matters might not be quite so straightforward.

Inability of insurance markets to provide the required service is one possible barrier. For insurers, the costs of monitoring the behaviour of those buying policies may be very high. The proposal that clients take over from architects liability for defects in buildings means that it would be much more difficult, and therefore costly, for insurers to assess the risk to which a client is exposed than to assess the risk to which a professional practice is exposed. Thus although it is expensive at present for clients to meet, indirectly, the indemnity insurance costs of architects, it would be much more expensive for them if they had to take out first party cover.

By the same token, NHS patients could buy personal accident insurance covering them, say, for loss of earnings if medical treatment fails. But this would not be a good way of controlling the quality of medical care because it would be impracticable, with current technology, to tailor premiums in such a way as to generate the right signals for doctors. Whilst different insurance arrangements might in principle be capable of producing the right pattern of compensation for victims they might be quite different in their capacity to generate the appropriate efficiency signals.

It has to be conceded that the negligence system may produce some undesirable effects. Victims with similar injuries may be compensated quite differently, and this contravenes one of the basic principles which, arguably, ought to be embodied in compensation schemes. A good example comes from treatment that produces serious, unanticipated deleterious side effects. Once this fact is established the treatment in question will no longer be regarded as a reasonable way of treating patients. Those injured by such treatment will be able to recover damages against a practitioner only if they received treatment after a certain date. This can look arbitrary and unfair from a victim's perspective although to the hard-nosed economist it is the only way of encouraging doctors to keep themselves informed about the consequences of different treatments.

Similar sorts of argument surround strict liability or 'no-fault' schemes. Victims suffering similar injuries may be treated differently under a negligence rule because in some cases the harm can be shown to be the consequence of a practitioner's failure to exercise a reasonable degree of care whilst in others it cannot. Again, we would caution against moves to strict liability as a way of remedying these apparent shortcomings on equity grounds until it can be shown that any efficiency loss would be limited.

This caveat would apply particularly strongly in circumstances where there is a prospect of compensation levels to victims being held artificially low so as to limit expenditure. For example, under a no-fault scheme for victims of medical accidents the rise in the number of persons claiming would be such that the only way of containing expenditure would be to impose quite modest ceilings on the amount of compensation recoverable. The merits of such a scheme, even on pure equity grounds, are dubious. From an efficiency perspective the dangers could be very great, since errors with catastrophic effects on victims would become less costly to those providing the service, making them less attentive to patients' needs.

Another important influence on the degree to which victims are compensated for losses under the negligence system is that of access to litigation. It is often argued that the poor can have legal aid, the rich can afford to pay but the group in the middle are effectively denied access. Differences in the terms of access will clearly be reflected in the number and kind of claims which are brought.

It is worth remembering that those clients who bring negligence actions contribute to a system which generates information and 'ensures' the quality of service for other clients. The benefits of litigation go beyond the compensation received by the client. Such litigants help to redress a potential market failure which arises because of the difficulty of monitoring and ensuring standards of quality. To this end, the informational flows that are generated by litigation can be seen as creating external benefits for all other clients of professional services.

Since there are external benefits of litigation there is good reason to ensure ease of access to litigation. Policy reform designed to attain this goal is then defensible on efficiency grounds. This is not to say that the potential litigant should not incur any cost; not all of the benefits of court actions are external. However this does offer support for recommendations, such those of the King's Fund (Ham et al., 1988a), which were discussed in Chapter 2. Greater advertising would provide plaintiffs with the means to select solicitors with specialised skills. Fee-splitting arrangements between solicitors would create incentives for solicitors to pass on cases to appropriate specialists. Recent experience has shown how important specialist advocacy has become. In the Blackburn case (BMJ, 1988), the plaintiff was advised by two sets of solicitors to settle for sums far below the costs finally awarded when his case was presented by a more specialist advocate.

The use of 'contingency fee' arrangements is another policy reform worth closer consideration. This practice, which operates in the USA, is one whereby lawyers' fees are only paid by clients when cases are successful. In the USA the person with a claim agrees with the lawyer the percentage of the damages he can keep in lieu of a fee. The lawyer may take anywhere between 25 per cent and 50 per cent of the award, and thus has a very clear incentive to get the highest amount of damages possible for the client. The risk of litigation is transferred from the client to the lawyer and, as the lawyer is likely to be better informed, there is good reason to believe that this encourages efficiency (Bowles 1982). The lawyer will, in any event, generally be better placed to take the risk than the client. By taking on a number of cases he is better able to diversify the risk attached to any single claim.

In the USA the system has been criticised because it is alleged that it turns lawyers into 'ambulance chasers'. Certainly lawyers have an incentive to find those cases which are most likely to succeed but by analogy they are unlikely to be interested in cases with little merit. It is then arguable whether this selection process, which brings forward the most obvious cases of negligence, is in the 'public interest' in so far as the information generated would be of advantage to other consumers. Whether the arrangement would increase the number of cases heard is difficult to ascertain, though it is likely to improve access for those cases where redress is important.

Recent proposals (in 1989) by the Lord Chancellor, Lord Mackay, to introduce contingency fees in England have to be treated with care. The proposal is for a variant of contingency fees based on the Scottish model, whereby the client pays no fee if he loses. Whilst this has the desired effect of eliminating one of the prospective litigant's greatest worries, the system is not widely used in Scotland. This is largely, it is thought, because the client remains responsible for the costs of the defendant if he loses. Thus while anyone bringing an unsuccessful claim will not be hit quite as hard as they are at present, they will certainly not enjoy the same degree of insulation from costs as their American counterpart.

The King's Fund study (Ham *et al.*, 1988*b*) recommends making access to legal aid easier. Legal aid has been defended generally on equity grounds i.e. enabling greater access to the law for low income groups. Here, for negligence cases, it can be defended on efficiency grounds, creating information which benefits other consumers. There is then a good case for consideration of increased public subsidy though there are, of course, alternative arrangements which may be employed. Moreover, such subsidy would be better targetted at those cases with merit and contingency arrangements between plaintiff and the state may have much to recommend them.

## 5.4   Administrative and Transactions Costs

The costs of operating a negligence system are currently very high. (See estimates of the administrative and legal costs of dealing with cases of medical malpractice in Chapter 2.) The transactions cost of the tort system are unquestionably high and one of the main arguments for moving to a system of no-fault would be to reduce these costs. For example, the costs of administering the social security system are very much lower in relation to the amounts paid through the system than they are for the negligence system. We have already demonstrated, as we repeat for convenience in Figure 5.1, that, in an 'idealised setting', a negligence action would minimise the sum of damage costs and resource costs of professional care. However, the missing element in this diagram is the transactions costs of administering the system.

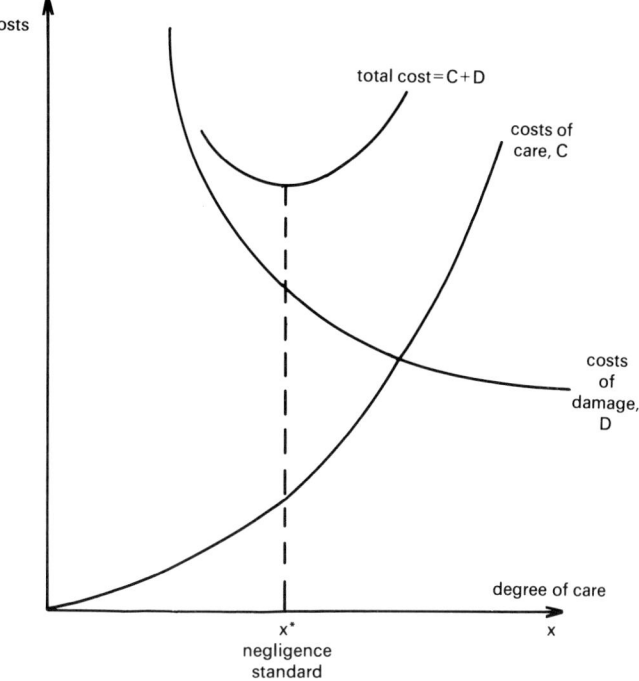

Figure 5.1    Efficient care and the negligence standard

While we have already recognised this problem explicitly in the estimates presented, we are still sceptical that a no-fault arrangement would be preferable to the current negligence system, for the following reasons:

(1) The question of no-fault is by no means as clear cut as it sounds. For example, in medicine under no-fault there would be a resource saving, in as much as there would no longer be a need to prove negligence. However, there would certainly be a requirement to prove that injury resulted from treatment, rather than simply from the nature of the medical ailment. It is not the case that no-fault should be equated with an open cheque book which covers all eventualities. Limitations would still need to be applied and hence cases would still require to be proven.

(2) There are steps which could be considered to reduce the existing costs of the tort system. For claims of negligence involving small sums it is particularly worrying that their amount may, at the end of the day, conceivably be less than the joint costs of prosecution and defence. For such cases there may be good reason to adopt an arbitration scheme (Jackson, 1988), the Solicitors' Arbitration Scheme being an example. Here each party pays a fixed sum for the arbitration. Written statements and copies of the relevant documents are provided by each side. The arbitrator will have sufficient

professional experience to decide the case. Whether, in extending this process, need exists for greater lay representation and judicial review is a matter for debate. However Jackson (1988, p 541) argues that: 'It is certainly my experience that a pair of arbitrators, one a lawyer and the other a professional person experienced in the subject matter of the dispute, makes an extremely effective tribunal'. By providing a more cost effective mechanism for small claims, it may be possible to reduce the administrative and transactions costs of the current system.

(3) The argument developed in this chapter is that the administrative and transactions costs are the 'price of information'. Moreover, it is the means by which the informational asymmetry between producer and consumer with respect to quality of care is redressed. With no-fault, would the educative and deterrent role of the system be lost, as is suggested by empirical analysis of no-fault systems (Landes, 1982)? Would this lead to a greater number of cases of negligence and to greater injustice? If so, should we simply realise that information is worth having even if there is a cost?

The search for an optimal procedure to deal with professional liability has to continue. The important conclusion from this analysis of four professions is that the behaviour of professional practitioners has been influenced by decisions by the courts on negligence claims. Present arrangements can be reformed, in terms of access and in terms of reducing transactions costs, so as to increase the sensitivity of practice to errors. Such reform need not damage significantly the educative and deterrent function of the tort system. But other calls for reform, particularly those which begin with the thesis that compensation to victims is not properly served by negligence, may contain serious dangers. Such schemes, by their focus on the victim, often ignore the cause of accidents and thereby run the danger of weakening the signal to the professional to go carefully. The net result can be greater inequity and higher total costs.

# Appendix     Sample of a Professional Indemnity Proposal Form for Accountants

Nelson Hurst & Marsh Ltd.
1 Seething Lane
London EC3N 4NH
Telephone: 01-4819090
Telex: 883756
Facsimile Copying Machine: 01-4819450

**STRICTLY PRIVATE
AND CONFIDENTIAL**

1. Name (s) of the Firm(s)

2. Address(es)

3. (a)  When was (were) the Firm(s) established?
   (b)  Is (Are) the Firm(s) admitted to membership of any Association?   **Yes/No**
        (If 'yes' please give details).

   (c)  Has (Have) the name(s) of the present Firm(s) been changed in the
        past 5 years or has any amalgamation taken place during this
        period? (If 'yes', please give details).                        **Yes/No**

4. Please give details of the Partners of the Firm(s) named above:
        Name              Qualifications        Date Qualified

5. Please give details of numbers of Staff
        (a)  Partners                                                   (a)
        (b)  Qualified Assistants/Consultants                           (b)
        (c)  Other Staff                                                (c)
   N.B. Omit Ancillary staff such as cleaners, lift attendants, drivers and
   the like.

6. Do you require cover for claims made against any independent
   accountant to whom work is subcontracted? If so, please identify:   **Yes/No**
        Name              Qualifications        Fees Paid
                                                (last financial year)

73

If 'Yes', please explain what controls the Firm(s) maintain over such sub-contracted work.

7. Do you require cover for any Partner for Liability arising out of a previous business? If so, please give: **Yes/No**

        Name      Name of previous practice      Date of leaving previous Practice

8. (a) Total gross fees for   19 /   19 /   19 /   19 /   19 /
      the last five financial
      years        £——  £——  £——  £——  £——

  (b) Financial year ends ————————

  (c) Of the above, please indicate the approximate percentage for each of the following categories in the last two years.

| | 19 | 19 |
|---|---|---|
| (i) Audit, Accountancy and Company Tax | ——% | ——% |
|   (a) Quoted Companies | ——% | ——% |
|   (b) Unquoted Companies | ——% | ——% |
|   (c) Others (including farmers, small traders, etc.) | ——% | ——% |
| (ii) Taxation only | ——% | ——% |
| (iii) Management Consultancy | ——% | ——% |
| (iv) Consultancy only | ——% | ——% |
| (v) Secretarial and Share Registration | ——% | ——% |
| (vi) Executorships and Trusteeship | ——% | ——% |
| (vii) Insolvencies, Liquidations and Receiverships | ——% | ——% |
| (viii) Insurance, Building Society and Stock Exchange Commissions | ——% | ——% |
| (ix) Directorships | ——% | ——% |
| (x) Entertainment/Leisure Industry | ——% | ——% |
| (xii) Any other—please give full details | ——% | ——% |
| | 100% | 100% |

  (d) Largest total fee from any one client or group in the last two financial years    £——  £——

  (e) Estimated total gross fees for the current financial year  £——

  (f) Do you conduct business for overseas clients?  **Yes/No**
     (If 'Yes', please give details.)

9. Are you currently insured for Professional Indemnity?
     If 'Yes' (a) What is the expiry date thereof?
           (b) Who are your present Insurers?
           (c) (i) Is there any Retroactive Limitation?  **Yes/No**
              (ii) If 'Yes', please state date  ————

**Explanatory Note re Q.9(c)**
The purport of this question is to establish whether your existing Insurers have imposed any limitation whereby claims will be admitted ONLY where the circumstances giving rise to such claim occured on or after a specified date. If such a limitation has been imposed it will be clearly endorsed, showing the date, on your policy.

10. Total Indemnity required £———

11. Please indicate the amount of any excess you are willing to bear £———

12. This insurance covers direct pecuniary loss sustained by the Insured as a result of fraud or dishonesty on the part of past or presnt Partners, Directors or employees of the Firm(s). As such, please answer the following:

    (a) Have any losses been sustained by fraud or dishonesty? **Yes/No**

    (b) Are you aware of any fraud or dishonesty on the part of past or present Partners or employees? **Yes/No**

    (c) Do you always take up **written** references when engaging staff **Yes/No**

    (d) Has any employee the authority to issue cheques bearing his signature alone? **Yes/No**

    (e) If the answer to the above is 'Yes', up to what amount? £———

    (f) Are the cash books of the firm(s) checked against Bank Statements independently of the Chief Cashier, Book-Keeper or (in the case of Insolvency Appointments) Manager? **Yes/No**

    (g) If the answer to the above is 'Yes', how frequently?

13. Is it the policy of the Firm(s) to obtain engagement letters from all clients? **Yes/No**
If 'No', please explain.
If 'Yes', please attach specimen.

14 Do you have separate insurance arrangements for physical loss of or damage to your property and/or the property of others in your care, custody or control? **Yes/No**

15. (a) Have any claims been made against the Firm(s) or their predecessors in business or any past or present Partners? (If 'Yes', please give details below). **Yes/No**

    (b) If so, has (have) the Firm(s) notified such claims to its Insurer? **Yes/No**

16. Are the Partners, **AFTER HAVING MADE FULL ENQUIRIES** aware of any of the following matters: (if 'yes', please give details below)?

    (a) Any circumstances which may give rise to a claim or claims against the firm, its predecessors in business or any past or present partner; **Yes/No**

    (b) the receipt of any complaints whether oral or in writing regarding services performed or advice given by the firm or on behalf of the firm; **Yes/No**

    (c) any loss of losses or potential loss or losses sustained by the firm arising from the loss or destruction of or damage to any books, documents or other property. **Yes/No**

17. Have any of the firms or persons named in answer to questions 1, 3 and 4 above at any time been refused similar insurance or quoted an **Yes/No**

increased premium or had special terms imposed? (If 'yes', please give details below).

18. **This space may be used to provide additional information (especially as regards Questions 3(b), 3(c), 8(b), 12, 15, 16 & 17).**

### THIS SECTION TO BE COMPLETED BY SOLE PRACTITIONERS ONLY

(1)  Are you in full time practice?

(2)  Age

(3)  Full experience of any assistants and length of service with you

(4)  (a)   What arrangements do you make when you are unable to attend your business?

     (b)   Do you have any agreement with any other firm to assist you when you are away? If so please give brief details.

**I/WE HEREBY DECLARE THAT THE ANSWERS GIVEN AND INFORMATION DISCLOSED IN THIS PROPOSAL ARE TRUE AND THAT NO MATERIAL FACTS HAVE BEEN MIS-STATED OR WITHHELD AND I/WE FURTHER AGREE THAT THIS PROPOSAL SHALL FORM THE BASIS OF THE CONTRACT BETWEEN ME/US AND THE INSURERS AND SHALL BE DEEMED TO BE INCORPORATED THERIN.**

Signed for and on behalf of the Firm(s) named in Question 1.

_____ (Senior Partner)

Dated in --------------this ---------------------day  of-----19-------------

# References

Akerlof, G (1970), 'The Market for Lemons: Qualitative Uncertainty and the Market Mechanism', *Quarterly Journal of Economics* vol 84, pp 488–500.

Arrow K J (1963), 'Uncertainty and the economics of medical care', *American Economic Review*, vol 53, p 941.

Bolt, D (1989) 'Compensating for Medical Mishaps—a model "no-fault" scheme', *New Law Journal*, 27 January 1989, pp 109–10.

Bowles, R (1982), *Law and the Economy* (Oxford: Martin Robertson).

Bowles, R and Jones, P (1988), 'Medical negligence and the allocation of health resources', *Professional Negligence*, vol 4 no 4, July/August 1988, pp 111–15.

Bowles, R and Jones, P (1989a), 'Medical negligence: A Health Authority's experience', *New Law Journal*, vol 139, no 6392, 27 January 1989.

Bowles, R and Jones, P (1989b), 'Rising Costs of Claims', *Health Service Journal*, 9 March 1989, pp 294–5.

Bowles, R and Jones, P (1989c), 'Medical indemnity insurance in the UK: a public choice approach', *The Geneva Papers on Risk and Insurance* (forthcoming).

Bowles, R and Jones, P (1989d), 'Medical negligence and resource allocation in the NHS: market versus non-market solutions', *Social Policy and Administration* (forthcoming).

Calabresi, G (1970), *Costs of Accidents* (New Haven: Yale University Press).

Cecil, Ray (1984), *Professional Liability* (London: Architectural Press Ltd).

Danzon, P M (1985), *Medical Malpractice* (Cambridge Mass and London: Harvard University Press).

Ham, C Dingwall, R, Fenn, P and Harris, D (1988a), *Medical Negligence: Compensation and Accountability*, Briefing Paper 6 Centre for Socio-Legal Studies, Oxford and the King's Fund Institute London.

Ham, C, Dingwall R, and Fenn, P (1988b), 'Improve health the no-fault way', *The Guardian*, 9 September, p 39.

Harris, D *et al.* (1984) *Compensation and Support for Illness and Injury* (Oxford, Clarendon Press).

Hawkins, C and Paterson, I (1987), 'Medicolegal audit in the West Midlands region: analysis of 100 cases', *British Medical Journal*, vol 295, pp 1533–6.

Hay, S (1987), *Are You Negligent? A Guide to Professional Liability and Indemnity Options* (London: The Economist Publications, Special Report No 1097).

Jackson, R (1988), 'Professional liability', *Royal Society of Arts Journal,* July 1988, pp 536–46.

Jensen, M and Meckling, W (1976) 'Theory of the Firm: Managerial Behaviour, Agency Costs and Ownership Structure', *Journal of Financial Economics*, 3, pp 305–60.

Landes, E (1982) 'Insurance, Liability and Accidents: a theoretical and empirical investigation of the effect of no-fault on accidents', *Journal of Law and Economics*, 25, pp 49–65.

Law Society (1979) *The Future of the Indemnity Insurance Scheme* (London: Law Society).

Law Society (1982) *A Consultative Document on the Future Basis of Premium Assessment* (London: Law Society).

Law Society (1984) *Statistical Bulletin,* various years (London: Law Society).

Law Society's Gazette (1987) 'A Smooth Transition'—an outline of the statutory fund which will replace the master policy on 1 September 1987.

Law Society (1988) *Solicitors' Indemnity Rules 1988* (London: Law Society).

McKenna, C J (1986), *The Economics of Uncertainty* (Brighton: Wheatsheaf).

Miller, F H (1986) 'Medical malpractice litigation: do the British have a better remedy?' *American Journal of Law and Medicine,* 11(4), pp 433–63.

Pearson Commission (1978) *Royal Commission on Civil Liability and Compensation for Personal Injury,* Cmnd 7054-I, London, HMSO.

Quam, L, Fenn, P and Dingwall, R (1987), 'Medical malpractice in perspective', *British Medical Journal,* vol 294, pp 1529–33 and pp 1597–1600.

Quam, L, Dingwall, R and Fenn, P (1988) 'Medical malpractice claims in obstetrics and gynaecology: comparisons between the United States and Britain', *British Journal of Obstetrics and Gynaecology* vol 95.

Schwartz, W B and Komesar, N K (1978), 'Doctors, damages and deterrence: an economic view of medical malpractice', *New England Journal of Medicine,* 298, 1282–9.

Shavell, S (1987) *Economic Analysis of Accident Law* (Harvard University Press: Cambridge, Mass).

Stephen, F H (1988) *The Economics of the Law* (Wheatsheaf Books: Brighton).

Warden, J (1987) 'Damages unlimited', *British Medical Journal,* vol 295, p 280.

Williamson, O E (1967) *Economics of Discretionary Behaviour: Managerial Objectives in a Theory of the Firm* (Chicago: Markham Publishing).

# THE DAVID HUME INSTITUTE

The David Hume Institute was established as a company limited by guarantee in January 1985, and it is registered as a charity. Its registration number in Scotland is 91239.

The objects of the Institute are to promote discourse and research on the economic and legal aspects of public policy questions.

## HUME PAPERS

1  Banking Deregulation *Michael Fry*
2  Reviewing Industrial Aid Programmes:
   (1) The Invergordon Smelter Case *Alex Scott and Margaret Cuthbert*
3  Sex at Work: Equal Pay and the "Comparable Worth" Controversy *Peter Sloane*
4  The European Communities' Common Fisheries Policy: A Critique *Antony W Dnes*
5  The Privatisation of Defence Supplies *Gavin Kennedy*
6  The Political Economy of Tax Evasion *David J Pyle*
7  Monopolies, Mergers and Restrictive Practices: UK Competition Policy 1948–87 *E Victor Morgan*

Published by **Aberdeen University Press**
8  The Small Entrepreneurial Firm *Gavin C Reid and Lowell R Jacobsen*
9  How Should Health Services be Financed? *Allan Massie*
10 Strategies for Higher Education—The Alternative White Paper *John Barnes and Nicholas Barr*
11 Professional Liability *Roger Bowles and Philip Jones*
12 Deregulation and the Future of Commercial Television *Gordon Hughes and David Vines*
13 The Ethics of Business *Norman Barry*
14 Copyright, Competition and Industrial Design *Hector MacQueen*
15 Student Loans *Nicholas Barr*
16 Agathotopia: The Economics of Partnership *James E Meade*